D1380202

Operational Level

Subject F1

Financial Reporting and Taxation

EXAM PRACTICE KIT

Published by: Kaplan Publishing UK

Unit 2 The Business Centre, Molly Millars Lane, Wokingham, Berkshire RG41 2QZ

Notice

British Library Cataloguing in Publication Data

A catalogue record for this book is available from the British Library

ISBN: 978-1-78415-545-2

Printed and bound in Great Britain

CONTENTS

	Page

Section

Quality and accuracy are of the utmost importance to us so if you spot an error in any of our products, please send an email to mykaplanreporting@kaplan.com with full details.

Our Quality Co-ordinator will work with our technical team to verify the error and take action to ensure it is corrected in future editions.

INDEX TO QUESTIONS AND ANSWERS

OBJECTIVE TEST QUESTIONS

EXAM TECHNIQUES

COMPUTER-BASED ASSESSMENT

TEN GOLDEN RULES

1   Make sure you have completed the compulsory 15 minute tutorial before you start exam. This tutorial is available through the CIMA website. You cannot speak to the invigilator once you have started.

2   These exam practice kits give you plenty of exam style questions to practise so make sure you use them to fully prepare.

3   Attempt all questions, there is no negative marking.

4   Double check your answer before you put in the final answer although you can change your response as many times as you like.

5   On multiple choice questions (MCQs), there is only one correct answer.

6   Not all questions will be MCQs – you may have to fill in missing words or figures.

7   Identify the easy questions first and get some points on the board to build up your confidence.

8   Try and allow 15 minutes at the end to check your answers and make any corrections.

9   If you don't know the answer, flag the question and attempt it later. In your final review before the end of the exam try a process of elimination.

10   Work out your answer on the whiteboard provided first if it is easier for you. There is also an onscreen 'scratch pad' on which you can make notes. You are not allowed to take pens, pencils, rulers, pencil cases, phones, paper or notes.

SYLLABUS GUIDANCE, LEARNING OBJECTIVES AND VERBS

A AIMS OF THE SYLLABUS

The aims of the syllabus are

- to provide for the Institute, together with the practical experience requirements, an adequate basis for assuring society that those admitted to membership are competent to act as management accountants for entities, whether in manufacturing, commercial or service organisations, in the public or private sectors of the economy

- to enable the Institute to examine whether prospective members have an adequate knowledge, understanding and mastery of the stated body of knowledge and skills

- to complement the Institute's practical experience and skills development requirements.

B STUDY WEIGHTINGS

A percentage weighting is shown against each topic in the syllabus. This is intended as a guide to the proportion of study time each topic requires.

All component learning outcomes will be tested and one question may cover more than one component learning outcome.

The weightings do not specify the number of marks that will be allocated to topics in the examination.

C LEARNING OUTCOMES

Each topic within the syllabus contains a list of learning outcomes, which should be read in conjunction with the knowledge content for the syllabus. A learning outcome has two main purposes:

1   to define the skill or ability that a well-prepared candidate should be able to exhibit in the examination

2   to demonstrate the approach likely to be taken by examiners in examination questions.

The learning outcomes are part of a hierarchy of learning objectives. The verbs used at the beginning of each learning outcome relate to a specific learning objective, e.g. Evaluate alternative approaches to budgeting.

The verb 'evaluate' indicates a high-level learning objective. As learning objectives are hierarchical, it is expected that at this level students will have knowledge of different budgeting systems and methodologies and be able to apply them.

A list of the learning objectives and the verbs that appear in the syllabus learning outcomes and examinations follows and these will help you to understand the depth and breadth required for a topic and the skill level the topic relates to.

Learning objectives	Verbs used	Definition
1 Knowledge		
What you are expected to know	List	Make a list of
	State	Express, fully or clearly, the details of/facts of
	Define	Give the exact meaning of
2 Comprehension		
What you are expected to understand	Describe	Communicate the key features of
	Distinguish	Highlight the differences between
	Explain	Make clear or intelligible/State the meaning of
	Identify	Recognise, establish or select after consideration
	Illustrate	Use an example to describe or explain something
3 Application		
How you are expected to apply your knowledge	Apply	To put to practical use
	Calculate/compute	To ascertain or reckon mathematically
	Demonstrate	To prove with certainty or to exhibit by practical means
	Prepare	To make or get ready for use
	Reconcile	To make or prove consistent/compatible
	Solve	Find an answer to
	Tabulate	Arrange in a table
4 Analysis		
How you are expected to analyse the detail of what you have learned	Analyse	Examine in detail the structure of
	Categorise	Place into a defined class or division
	Compare and contrast	Show the similarities and/or differences between
	Construct	To build up or compile
	Discuss	To examine in detail by argument
	Interpret	To translate into intelligible or familiar terms
	Produce	To create or bring into existence
5 Evaluation		
How you are expected to use your learning to evaluate, make decisions or recommendations	Advise	To counsel, inform or notify
	Evaluate	To appraise or assess the value of
	Recommend	To advise on a course of action
	Advise	To counsel, inform or notify

D OBJECTIVE TEST

The most common types of Objective Test questions are:

- multiple choice, where you have to choose the correct answer(s) from a list of possible answers. This could either be numbers or text

- multiple choice with more choices and answers – for example, choosing two correct answers from a list of eight possible answers. This could either be numbers or text

- single numeric entry, where you give your numeric answer e.g. profit is $10,000

- multiple entry, where you give several numeric answers e.g. the charge for electricity is $2000 and the accrual is $200

- true/false questions, where you state whether a statement is true or false e.g. external auditors report to the directors is FALSE

- matching pairs of text e.g. the convention 'prudence' would be matched with the statement' inventories revalued at the lower of cost and net realisable value'

- other types could be matching text with graphs and labelling graphs/diagrams.

In this Exam Practice Kit we have used these types of questions.

Some further guidance from CIMA on number entry questions is as follows:

- For number entry questions, you do not need to include currency symbols or other characters or symbols such as the percentage sign, as these will have been completed for you. You may use the decimal point but must not use any other characters when entering an answer (except numbers) so, for example, $10,500.80 would be input as 10500.80.

- When expressing a decimal, for example a probability or correlation coefficient, you should include the leading zero (i.e. you should input 0.5 not .5).

- Negative numbers should be input using the minus sign, for example −1000.

- You will receive an error message if you try to enter a character or symbol that is not permitted (for example a '£' or '%' sign).

- A small range of answers will normally be accepted, taking into account sensible rounding.

Guidance re CIMA On-Screen calculator:

As part of the computer based assessment software, candidates are now provided with a calculator. This calculator is on-screen and is available for the duration of the assessment. The calculator is accessed by clicking the calculator button in the top left hand corner of the screen at any time during the assessment.

All candidates must complete a 15 minute tutorial before the assessment begins and will have the opportunity to familiarise themselves with the calculator and practise using it.

Candidates may practise using the calculator by downloading and installing the practice exam at http://www.vue.com/athena/. The calculator can be accessed from the fourth sample question (of 12).

Please note that the practice exam and tutorial provided by Pearson VUE at http://www.vue.com/athena/ is not specific to CIMA and includes the full range of question types the Pearson VUE software supports, some of which CIMA does not currently use.

The Objective Tests are ninety minute computer-based assessments comprising 60 compulsory questions, with one or more parts. CIMA is continuously developing the question styles within the system and you are advised to try the online website demo at www.cimaglobal.com, to both gain familiarity with assessment software and examine the latest style of questions being used.

APPROACH TO REVISION

Stage 1: Assess areas of strengths and weaknesses

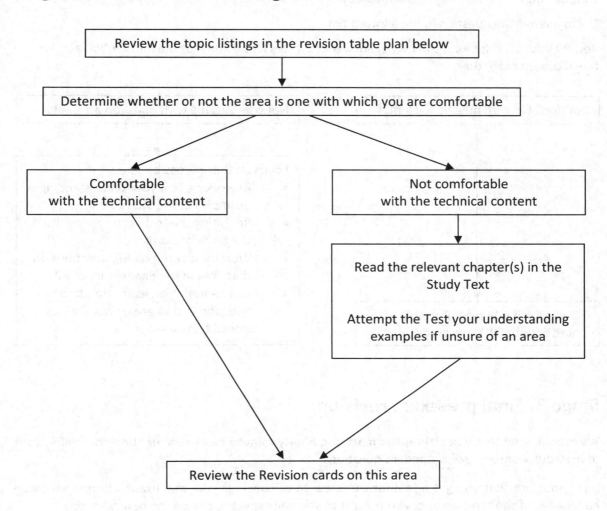

Review the topic listings in the revision table plan below

Determine whether or not the area is one with which you are comfortable

Comfortable
with the technical content

Not comfortable
with the technical content

Read the relevant chapter(s) in the
Study Text

Attempt the Test your understanding
examples if unsure of an area

Review the Revision cards on this area

Stage 2: Question practice

Follow the order of revision of topics as recommended in the revision table plan below and attempt the questions in the order suggested.

Try to avoid referring to text books and notes and the model answer until you have completed your attempt.

Try to answer the question in the allotted time.

Review your attempt with the model answer and assess how much of the answer you achieved in the allocated exam time.

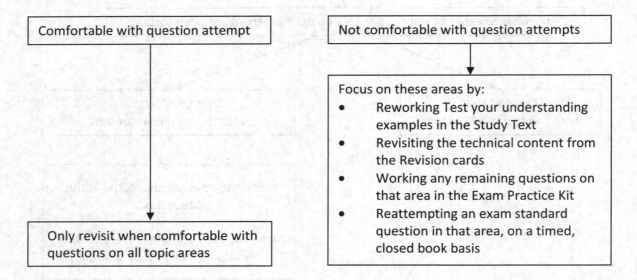

Stage 3: Final pre-exam revision

We recommend that you **attempt at least one ninety minute mock examination** containing a set of previously unseen exam standard questions.

It is important that you get a feel for the breadth of coverage of a real exam without advanced knowledge of the topic areas covered – just as you will expect to see on the real exam day.

Ideally a mock examination offered by your tuition provider should be sat in timed, closed book, real exam conditions.

F1
FINANCIAL REPORTING AND TAXATION

Syllabus overview

F1 covers the regulation and preparation of financial statements and how the information contained in them can be used. It provides the competencies required to produce financial statements for both individual entities and groups using appropriate international financial reporting standards. It also gives insight into how to effectively source and manage cash and working capital, which are essential for both the survival and success of organisations. The final part focuses on the basic principles and application of business taxation. The competencies gained from F1 form the basis for developing further insights into producing and analysing complex group accounts (covered in F2) and formulating and implementing financial strategy (covered in F3).

Summary of syllabus

Weight	Syllabus topic
10%	A. Regulatory environment for financial reporting and corporate governance
45%	B. Financial accounting and reporting
20%	C. Management of working capital, cash and sources of short-term finance
25%	D. Fundamentals of business taxation

F1 – A. REGULATORY ENVIRONMENT FOR FINANCIAL REPORTING AND CORPORATE GOVERNANCE (10%)

Learning outcomes
On completion of their studies, students should be able to:

Lead	Component	Indicative syllabus content
1 explain the need for and the process of regulating the financial reporting information of incorporated entities.	(a) explain the need for the regulation of the financial reporting information of incorporated entities and the key elements of an ethical regulatory environment for such information	• The need for the regulation of financial reporting information. • Key elements of the regulatory environment for financial reporting including local corporate law, local and international conceptual frameworks, local and international financial reporting standards and other regulatory bodies. • Sources of professional codes of ethics. • Provisions of the CIMA Code of Ethics for Professional Accountants of particular relevance to the preparation of financial reporting information. • Rules-based versus principles-based approaches to accounting regulation.
	(b) explain the roles and structures of the key bodies involved in the regulation of financial reporting information	• Role and structure of: – The IFRS Foundation. – The International Accounting Standards Board (IASB). – IFRS Advisory Council. – IFRS Interpretations Committee. – International Organisation of Securities Commissions (IOSCO).
	(c) explain the scope of IFRS and how they are developed	• Interaction of local GAAP bodies with the IASB. • Scope of specific standards in specialised circumstances – IAS 26 *Accounting and Reporting by Retirement Benefit Plans*, IAS 41 *Agriculture*, IFRS 4 *Insurance Contracts*, IFRS 6 *Exploration for and Evaluation of Mineral Resources* and IFRS for SMEs (specific knowledge of these standards will not be tested). • The standard setting process for IFRS.

Learning outcomes
On completion of their studies, students should be able to:

Lead	Component	Indicative syllabus content
	(d) describe the role of the external auditor in the context of the financial reporting information of incorporated entities and the content and significance of the audit report.	• Powers and duties of external auditors. • Content of the audit report. • Types of audit report. • Significance of the audit report.
2 discuss the need for and key principles of corporate governance regulation.	(a) discuss the need for and scope of corporate governance regulation	• The need for corporate governance regulation. • Scope of corporate governance regulation.
	(b) compare and contrast the approach to corporate governance in different markets.	• Approach to corporate governance regulations in primary markets around the world, in particular the US and UK. • Key differences in approach across these markets.

F1 – B. FINANCIAL ACCOUNTING AND REPORTING (45%)

Learning outcomes
On completion of their studies, students should be able to:

Lead	Component	Indicative syllabus content

1 explain the main elements of and key principles underpinning financial statements prepared in accordance with international financial reporting standards.	(a) describe the main elements of financial statements prepared in accordance with IFRS	• Content of financial statements as specified in:
		  – preface to IFRS
		  – IAS 1 *Presentation of Financial Reporting*
		  – IAS 8 *Accounting Policies, Changes in Accounting Estimates and Errors*
		  – IAS 34 *Interim Financial Reporting*
		  – IFRS 8 *Operating Segments*.

	(b) explain the key principles contained within the IASB's Conceptual Framework for Financial Reporting.	• Key principles of the Conceptual Framework for Financial Reporting. • Broad principles of accounting for fair values (contained in IFRS 13 *Fair Value Measurement*).

2 produce the primary financial statements of an individual entity incorporating accounting transactions and adjustments, in accordance with relevant international financial reporting standards, in an ethical manner.	(a) produce the primary financial statements from trial balance for an individual entity in accordance with IFRS	• Production of the:
		  – statement of financial position
		  – statement of comprehensive income
		  – statement of changes in equity
		  – statement of cash flows
		  – for a single incorporated entity in accordance with IAS 1 *Presentation of Financial Reporting* and IAS 7 *Statement of Cash Flows*.

	(b) apply the rules contained in IFRS to generate appropriate accounting entries in respect of reporting performance, accounting for taxation, employee benefits, non-current assets, accounting for government grants, impairment, inventories and events after the reporting period	• Reporting performance – IFRS 5 *Non-current Assets Held for Sale and Discontinued Operations* and IAS 21 *The Effects of Changes in Foreign Exchange Rates* (individual transactions only). • Accounting for taxation – IAS 12 *Income Taxes* (not deferred tax). • Employee benefits – IAS 19 *Employee Benefits*. • Non-current assets – IAS 16 *Property, Plant and Equipment*, IAS 23 *Borrowing Costs*, IAS 38 *Intangible Assets*, IAS 40 *Investment Property*, and IFRS 5 *Non-current Assets Held for Sales and Discontinued Operations*.

Learning outcomes

On completion of their studies, students should be able to:

Lead	Component		Indicative syllabus content
			• Accounting for government grants – IAS 20 *Accounting for Government Grants and Disclosure of Government Assistance.* • Impairment – IAS 36 *Impairment of Assets.* • Inventories – IAS 2 *Inventories.* • Events after the reporting period – IAS 10 *Events after the Reporting Period.*
	(c)	discuss the ethical selection and adoption of relevant accounting policies and accounting estimates.	• Ethics in financial reporting in respect of selection and adoption of accounting policies and estimates.
3 produce the consolidated statement of financial position and consolidated statement of comprehensive income in accordance with relevant international financial reporting standards, in an ethical manner.	(a)	explain whether an investment in another entity constitutes a subsidiary or an associate relationship in accordance with relevant international financial reporting standards	• Provisions of IFRS 10 *Consolidated Financial Statements* and IAS 28 *Investments in Associates* in respect of power to control and significant influence.
	(b)	explain situations where a parent entity is exempt from preparing consolidated financial statements	• Exemptions from preparing consolidated financial statements, in accordance with IFRS 10 *Consolidated Financial Statements* and the requirements of IAS 27 *Separate Financial Statements.*
	(c)	produce the consolidated statement of financial position and statement of comprehensive income in accordance with relevant IFRS for a group comprising of one or more subsidiaries (being either wholly or partially directly owned) or associates, including interests acquired part way through an accounting period.	• Principles of full consolidation and equity accounting in accordance with IFRS 3 *Business Combinations* and IAS 28 *Investments in Associates.* • Production of: – consolidated statement of financial position – consolidated statement of comprehensive income.

Learning outcomes

On completion of their studies, students should be able to:

Lead	Component	Indicative syllabus content
		• Including the adoption of both full consolidation and the principles of equity accounting, in accordance with the provisions of IAS 1 *Presentation of Financial Statements*, IAS 28 *Investments in Associates*, IFRS 3 *Business Combinations* and IFRS 10 *Consolidated Financial Statements*. **Note:** Fair value adjustments in respect of assets and liabilities at acquisition will not be tested, however non-controlling interests at either fair value or share of net assets will be tested.

F1 – C. MANAGEMENT OF WORKING CAPITAL, CASH AND SOURCES OF SHORT-TERM FINANCE (20%)

Learning outcomes
On completion of their studies, students should be able to:

Lead	Component	Indicative syllabus content
1 describe the sources of short-term finance and cash investment.	(a) describe the sources of short-term finance and methods of short-term cash investment available to an entity.	• Types of short-term finance including trade payables, overdrafts, short-term loans and debt factoring. • Types of cash investment including interest-bearing deposits, short-term treasury bills and other securities.
2 evaluate the working capital position of an entity.	(a) analyse trade receivables, trade payables and inventory ratios	• Calculation of trade receivable, trade payable and inventory days. • Interpretation of the ratios either in comparison to prior periods, competitors or to the industry as a whole, taking into account the nature of the industry.
	(b) discuss policies for the management of the total level of investment in working capital and for the individual elements of working capital	• Working capital cycle. • Policies for the management of the total level of investment in working capital – aggressive, moderate and conservative. • Methods of trade receivables management, including credit control procedures. • Methods of trade payables management and significance of trade payables as a source of finance and how this affects the relationship with suppliers. • Methods of inventory management, including calculations of the economic order quantity (EOQ).
	(c) evaluate working capital policies	• Financial impact of changing working capital policies. • Impact and risks of overtrading. • Identification of areas for improvement.
	(d) discuss approaches to the financing of working capital investment levels.	• Approaches to the financing of the investment in working capital – aggressive, moderate and conservative.

Learning outcomes

On completion of their studies, students should be able to:

Lead	Component	Indicative syllabus content
3 analyse the short-term cash position of an entity.	(a) discuss measures to manage the short-term cash position of an entity.	<ul><li>Preparation of short-term cash flow forecasts.</li><li>Identification of surpluses or deficits from cash flow forecasts.</li><li>Selection of appropriate short-term solutions.</li><li>Principles of investing short term including maturity, return, security and liquidity.</li></ul>

F1 – D. FUNDAMENTALS OF BUSINESS TAXATION (25%)

Learning outcomes
On completion of their studies, students should be able to:

Lead	Component	Indicative syllabus content

1 discuss the types of taxation that typically apply to an incorporated entity and the regulatory environment for taxation.	(a) discuss the features of the types of indirect and direct taxation that typically apply to an incorporated entity	• Definitions of direct taxation, indirect taxation, taxable person, incidence and competent jurisdiction.
		• Types of taxation – progressive, proportional and regressive.
		• Features of the following types of indirect taxation:
		  – unit taxes
		  – ad valorem taxes
		  – excise duties
		  – property and wealth taxes
		  – consumption taxes
		  – mechanism of value added tax in the context of an incorporated entity.
		• Features of the following types of direct taxation:
		  – tax on trading income
		  – capital taxes.
		• Impact of employee taxation.

	(b) discuss the regulatory environment for taxation, including the distinction between tax evasion and tax avoidance.	• Sources of taxation rules such as domestic legislation, court rulings, domestic interpretations and guidelines, EU guidelines and taxation agreements between different countries. • Administration of taxation including the principles of record keeping, deadlines and penalties. • Powers of taxation authorities. • Distinction between tax evasion and tax avoidance and the ethical considerations faced by an entity in respect of tax avoidance.

Learning outcomes
On completion of their studies, students should be able to:

Lead	Component	Indicative syllabus content

2 explain the taxation issues that may apply to an incorporated entity that operates internationally.	(a) explain the taxation issues that may apply to an incorporated entity that operates internationally.	• International taxation issues:
		  – the concept of corporate residence and the key bases of determining residence
		  – types of overseas operations: subsidiary or branch and the implications of each on taxation
		  – issue of double taxation and the methods of gaining relief
		  – types of foreign taxation and the distinction between withholding tax and underlying tax (calculations will not be tested)
		  – transfer pricing and related, ethical and taxation issues.

3 produce computations for corporate income tax and capital tax.	(a) produce corporate income tax computations from a given set of rules	• Distinction between accounting profit and taxable profit and the reconciliation between them. This will include (based upon a set of rules given in the examination):
		  – identification and treatment of exempt income or income taxed under different rules
		  – identification and treatment of disallowable expenditure
		  – replacement of accounting depreciation with tax depreciation
		  – calculation of tax depreciation allowances
		  – calculation of corporate income tax liability
		  – relief for trading losses.

	(b) produce capital tax computations from a given set of rules.	• Principle of a capital tax computation on the sale of an asset. • Allowable costs. • Methods of relieving capital losses. • Concept of rollover relief.

TABLES

Information concerning formulae and tables will be provided via the CIMA website, www.cimaglobal.com and your EN-gage login.

Section 1

OBJECTIVE TEST QUESTIONS

FUNDAMENTALS OF BUSINESS TAX

1   Complete the sentence below by placing one of the following options in the space.

Competent jurisdiction is _____.

> the country whose tax laws apply to the entity
>
> the country the income arises in
>
> the country where the parent is incorporated

2   Complete the sentence below by placing one of the following options in the space.

A taxable person is _____.

> the person or entity who is responsible for completing the tax return
>
> the person or entity who accountable for the tax payment
>
> the person or entity who has direct contact with the tax authority

3   Which TWO of the following are methods used for double tax relief?

A   Exemption relief

B   Deduction relief

C   Tax loss relief

D   Withholding relief

E   Underlying relief

4   Which of the following could be said to be a progressive tax?

A   Property sales tax of 1% of the selling price of all properties sold

B   Value added tax at a rate of 0%, 10% or 15% depending on the type of goods or services provided

C   Corporate wealth tax at 2% of total net assets up to $10 million then at 0.5% on net assets greater than $10 million

D   Personal income tax of 10% on earnings up to $10,000, then at 15% from $10,001 up to $100,000 and 25% over $100,000

5 Complete the sentence below by placing one of the following options in the space.

Tax evasion is _____.

| a legal way of avoiding paying taxes |
| an illegal way of avoiding paying taxes |

6 An ideal tax system should conform to certain principles. Which of the following statements is NOT generally regarded as a principle of an ideal tax?

A   It should be fair to different individuals and should reflect a person's ability to pay

B   It should not be arbitrary, it should be certain

C   It should raise as much money as possible for the government

D   It should be convenient in terms of timing and payment

7 Complete the sentence below by placing one of the following options in the space.

A direct tax is one that _____.

| is passed onto another part of the economy |
| is imposed on the final consumer |
| is levied directly on the person who is intended to pay the tax |

8 Which of the following statements is NOT a source of tax rules in a country?

A   Domestic legislation

B   Directives from a supranational body

C   International treaties

D   International accounting standards

9 CR is resident in Country X. CR makes a taxable profit of $750,000 and pays an equity dividend of $350,000. CR pays tax on profits at a rate of 25%.

Equity shareholders pay tax on their dividend income at a rate of 30%.

If CR and its equity shareholders pay a total of $205,000 tax between them, what method of corporate income tax is being used in Country X?

A   The classical system

B   The imputation system

C   The partial imputation system

D   The split rate system

10 Which of the following is NOT a benefit of pay-as-you-earn (PAYE) method of tax collection?

A   It makes payment of tax easier for the tax payer as it is in instalments

B   It makes it easier for governments to forecast tax revenues

C   It benefits the tax payer as it reduces the tax payable

D   It improves government's cash flow as cash is received earlier

11   **Which of the following is NOT a reason for governments to set deadlines for filing tax returns and payment of taxes?**

   A   To enable governments to enforce penalties for late payments

   B   To ensure tax deducted at source by employers is paid over promptly

   C   To ensure tax payers know when they have to make payment

   D   To ensure that the correct amount of tax revenue is paid

12   **Which of the following powers is a tax authority least likely to have granted to them?**

   A   Power of arrest

   B   Power to examine records

   C   Power of entry and search

   D   Power to give information to other countries' tax authorities

13   The OECD model tax convention defines a permanent establishment to include a number of different types of establishments.

   Which TWO of the following are included in the OECD's list of permanent establishments?

   A   A place of management

   B   A warehouse

   C   A subsidiary

   D   A quarry

   E   A building site that was used for nine months

14   In Country Y, A earns $75,000 profit for the year and receives a tax bill for $17,000.

   B earns $44,000 profit for the year and receives a tax bill for $4,800.

   Country Y's income tax could be said to be a:

   A   Regressive tax

   B   Proportional tax

   C   Progressive tax

   D   Fixed rate tax

15   **Which THREE of the following statements are the main reasons why governments set deadlines for filing returns and/or paying taxes?**

   A   The tax authority is more likely to get paid on time

   B   The payment will be more accurate

   C   The costs to collect the tax will be less

   D   The tax administration will be easier

   E   The tax authorities can forecast their cash flows

   F   They can impose penalties for late payment/late filing

16   In 1776, Adam Smith proposed that an acceptable tax should meet four characteristics. Three of these characteristics were certainty, convenience and efficiency.

Identify the FOURTH characteristic.

A   Neutrality

B   Transparency

C   Equity

D   Simplicity

17   Country X uses a Pay-As-You-Earn (PAYE) system for collecting taxes from employees. Each employer is provided with information about each employee's tax position and tables showing the amount of tax to deduct each period. Employers are required to deduct tax from employees and pay it to the revenue authorities on a monthly basis.

From the perspective of the government, which THREE of the following statements are the main advantages of the PAYE system?

A   Tax is collected regularly throughout the year so easier to forecast spending

B   The administrative costs are largely passed to the employers

C   Tax calculations are more accurate than the self-assessment system

D   The administrative costs are largely passed to the employees

E   Tax is collected regularly throughout the year so easier than making a large payment

F   There is less risk of default as tax is deducted at source

18   **Place the THREE of the following options into the highlighted boxes in the table below to correctly reflect the characteristics of a commodity that, from a revenue authority's point of view, would make that commodity suitable for an excise duty to be imposed.**

| There are few large producers/suppliers |
| Demand is elastic with no close substitutes |
| Sales volumes are large |
| Demand is inelastic with no close substitutes |
| Sales volumes are small |
| There are many large producers/suppliers |

Suitable for excise duties

19 Tax deducted at source by employers from employees' earnings and paid to government, often called pay-as-you-earn (PAYE) has a number of advantages.

(i)   Most of the administration costs are borne by the employer.

(ii)   Employers may delay payment or fail to pay over PAYE deducted from employees.

(iii) Employers may be inefficient and not deduct any tax or deduct the wrong amount from employees.

(iv)   Government receives a higher proportion of the tax due as defaults and late payments are fewer.

Which TWO of the above are NOT likely to be seen as an advantage of PAYE by the government?

A   (i) and (ii)

B   (ii) and (iii)

C   (ii) and (iv)

D   (iii) and (iv)

20   **What is Hypothecation?**

A   Process of earmarking tax revenues for specific types of expenditure

B   Estimation of tax revenue made by the tax authorities for budget purposes

C   Refund made by tax authorities for tax paid in other countries

D   Payment of taxes due to tax authorities, net of tax refunds due from tax authorities

21   **The tax gap is the difference between:**

A   when a tax payment is due and the date it is actually paid

B   the tax due calculated by the entity and the tax demanded by the tax authority

C   the amount of tax due to be paid and the amount actually collected

D   the date when the entity was notified by the tax authority of the tax due and the date the tax should be paid

22   Developed countries generally use three tax bases. One tax base widely used is income.

What are the other TWO widely used tax bases?

A   Assets

B   Profit

C   Consumption

D   Salary

E   Earnings

23 **Which TWO of the following are most likely to encourage an increase in incidence of tax avoidance or tax evasion?**

    (i)   High penalties for tax evasion.

    (ii)   Imprecise and vague tax laws.

    (iii)   A tax system that is seen as fair to everyone.

    (iv)   Very high tax rates.

    A   (i) and (ii)

    B   (ii) and (iii)

    C   (ii) and (iv)

    D   (iii) and (iv)

24 **Which of the following is NOT an advantage for the tax authority of deduction of tax at source?**

    A   The total amount of tax due for the period is easier to calculate

    B   Tax is collected earlier

    C   Administration costs are borne by the entity deducting tax

    D   Tax is deducted before income is paid to the taxpayer

25 HD sells office stationery and adds a sales tax to the selling price of all products sold. A customer purchases goods from HD has to pay the cost of the goods plus the sales tax. HD pays the sales tax collected to the tax authorities.

From the perspective of HD the sales tax would be said to have:

    A   formal incidence

    B   effective incidence

    C   informal incidence

    D   ineffective incidence

26 **Which of the following defines the meaning of tax gap?**

    A   The difference between the tax an entity expects to pay and the amount notified by the tax authority

    B   The difference between the total amount of tax due to be paid and the amount actually collected by the tax authority

    C   The difference between the due date for tax payment and the date it is actually paid

    D   The difference between the amount of tax provided in the financial statements and the amount actually paid

27   **Which of the following would be considered to be an example of an indirect tax?**

A   An entity assessed for corporate income tax on its profit

B   An individual purchases goods in a shop, the price includes VAT

C   An employee has tax deducted from salary through the PAYE system

D   An individual pays capital gains tax on a gain arising on the disposal of an investment

28   Country Z has the following tax regulations in force for the years 20X5 and 20X6 (each year January to December):

- Corporate income is taxed at the following rates:

    - $1 to $10,000 at 0%

    - $10,001 to $25,000 at 15%

    - $25,001 and over at 25%.

- When calculating corporate income tax, Country Z does **not** allow the following types of expenses to be charged against taxable income:

    - entertaining expenses

    - taxes paid to other public bodies

    - accounting depreciation of non-current assets.

- Tax relief on capital expenditure is available at the following rates:

    - buildings at 4% per annum on straight line basis

    - all other non-current tangible assets are allowed tax depreciation at 27% per annum on reducing balance basis.

DB commenced business on 1 January 20X5 when all assets were purchased. No first year allowances were available for 20X5.

Non-current assets cost at 1 January 20X5

	$
Land	27,000
Buildings	70,000
Plant and equipment	80,000

On 1 January 20X6, DB purchased another machine for $20,000. This machine qualified for a first year tax allowance of 50%.

DB's Statement of profit or loss for the year to 31 December 20X6

	$
Gross profit	160,000
Administrative expenses	(81,000)
Entertaining	(600)
Tax paid to local government	(950)
Depreciation on buildings	(1,600)
Depreciation on plant and equipment	(20,000)
Distribution costs	(20,000)
	35,850
Finance cost	(1,900)
Profit before tax	33,950

Calculate DB's corporate income tax due for the year to 31 December 20X6.

$ _____. (Your answer should be rounded down to the nearest $.)

29 CFP, an entity resident in Country X, had an accounting profit for the year ended 31 December 20X1 of $860,000. The accounting profit was after charging depreciation of $42,000 and amortisation of development costs of $15,000 which should be treated as disallowable expenses.

CFP was entitled to a tax depreciation allowance of $51,000 for the year to 31 December 20X1.

Tax is charged at 25%.

CFP's tax payable for the year ended 31 December 20X1 is:

A $202,250

B $206,500

C $212,750

D $216,500

30   **Which of the following defines the meaning of hypothecation?**

A   A new tax law has to be passed each year to allow taxes to be legally collected

B   The difference between the total amount of tax due to be paid and the amount actually collected by the tax authority

C   Tax is deducted from amounts due before they are paid to the recipient

D   The products of certain taxes are devoted to specific types of public expenditure

31   **Which of the following would NOT normally be considered a principle of a modern tax system?**

A   Efficiency

B   Equity

C   Economic impact

D   Raise revenues

32   **Complete the sentence below by placing one of the following options in the space.**

Under the OECD model tax convention an entity will generally have residence for tax purposes in _____.

| the country of effective management |
| the country of incorporation |
| the country where most revenue is generated |

33   An entity earns a profit of $60,000 for the year to 31 March 20X2. The entity is assessed and owes $15,000 tax for the year.

Which of the following types of tax would best describe the tax due?

A   Capital tax

B   Income tax

C   Wealth tax

D   Consumption tax

34   **Place the TWO of the following options into the highlighted boxes in the table below to correctly reflect TWO possible powers that a tax authority may be granted to enable it to enforce tax regulations.**

| Power to review and query filed returns |
| Power to arrest |
| Power to enforce changes |
| Power to remove directors |
| Power to exchange information with tax authorities in other jurisdictions |

Powers of the tax authority

35   Taxes commonly used by many countries include:

(i)   import duty payable on specific types of imported goods

(ii)   individual income tax, usually deducted at source

(iii) corporate income tax

(iv)   value added tax.

Which of the above would normally be defined as direct taxation?

A   (i) and (ii)

B   (i) and (iv)

C   (ii) and (iii)

D   (ii) and (iv)

36   An entity makes a taxable profit of $500,000 and pays corporate income tax at 25%.

The entity pays a dividend to its shareholders. A shareholder receiving $5,000 dividend then pays the standard personal income tax rate of 15% on the dividend, paying a further $750 tax.

The tax system could be said to be:

A   A classical system

B   An Imputation system

C   A partial imputation system

D   A split rate system

37   Tax authorities use various methods to reduce tax avoidance and tax evasion.

(i)   Increase tax rates to compensate for losses due to evasion.

(ii)   Make the tax structure as complicated as possible.

(iii) Increase the perceived risk by auditing tax returns.

(iv)   Simplify the tax structure, minimising allowances and exemptions.

Which of the above methods could be used to help reduce tax evasion and avoidance?

A   (i) and (ii)

B   (i) and (iv)

C   (ii) and (iii)

D   (iii) and (iv)

38   **Complete the sentence below by placing one of the following options in the space.**

Tax avoidance is _____.

| a legal way of avoiding paying taxes |
| an illegal way of avoiding paying taxes |

39   Accounting depreciation is usually disallowed when calculating tax due by an entity and a deduction for tax depreciation is given instead.

   Which of the following statements explains the reason why accounting depreciation is replaced with tax depreciation in a tax computation?

   A   Tax depreciation gives the tax payer more relief than accounting depreciation

   B   Tax depreciation gives the tax payer less relief than accounting depreciation

   C   To ensure that all entities are allowed the same rates of depreciation for tax purposes

   D   To ensure that the tax authority raises as much tax as possible

40   **A customer purchases goods for $115, inclusive of VAT. From the customer's point of view the VAT could be said to be:**

   A   a direct tax with formal incidence

   B   an indirect tax with formal incidence

   C   a direct tax with effective incidence

   D   an indirect tax with effective incidence

41   Country X has the following tax regulations in force:

   ● The tax year is 1 May to 30 April.

   ● All corporate profits are taxed at 20%.

   ● When calculating corporate taxable income, depreciation of non-current assets cannot be charged against taxable income.

   ● Tax depreciation is allowed at the following rates:

      – buildings at 5% per annum on straight line basis

      – all other non-current tangible assets are allowed tax depreciation at 25% per annum on a reducing balance basis.

   No tax allowances are allowed on land or furniture and fittings.

   FB commenced trading on 1 May 20X5 when it purchased all its non-current assets.

   FB's non-current asset balances were:

	Cost 1 May 20X5	Carrying value 1 May 20X7	Tax written down value 1 May 20X7
	$	$	$
Land	20,000	20,000	–
Buildings	80,000	73,600	72,000
Plant and equipment	21,000	1,000	11,812
Furniture and fittings	15,000	5,000	–

   FB did not purchase any non-current assets between 1 May 20X5 and 30 April 20X7. On 2 May 20X7, FB disposed of all its plant and equipment for $5,000 and purchased new plant and equipment for $30,000. The new plant and equipment qualified for a first year tax allowance of 50%.

FB's Statement of profit or loss for the year ended 30 April 20X8

	$
Gross profit	210,000
Administrative expenses	(114,000)
Gain on disposal of plant and equipment	4,000
Depreciation – furniture and fittings	(5,000)
Depreciation – buildings	(3,200)
Depreciation – plant and equipment	(6,000)
Distribution costs	(49,000)
	36,800
Finance cost	(7,000)
Profit before tax	29,800

Calculate FB's corporate income tax due for the year ended 30 April 20X8.

$ _____. (Your answer should be rounded down to the nearest $.)

Data for Questions 42 and 43

Country Y has the following tax regulations in force:

- Corporate income is taxed at the rate of 25%.

- When calculating corporate income tax Country Y does not allow entertaining or accounting depreciation on non-current assets to be charged against taxable income.

The following is an extract from JW's statement of profit or loss for the year to 31 December 20X8:

	$
Revenue	669,000
Cost of sales	(320,000)
Gross profit	349,000
Administration expenses	(124,000)
Distribution costs	(30,000)
	195,000
Finance cost	(45,000)
Profit before tax	150,000

Cost of sales includes depreciation charges of $27,000 for property, plant and equipment. Distribution costs include a depreciation charge for a new vehicle (see below). Included in administration expenses are entertainment costs of $2,200.

On 1 January 20X8 JW purchased its first delivery vehicle for $12,000. The vehicle qualified for first year tax allowance of 40%. It had an estimated useful life of six years with no residual value.

The property, plant and equipment qualified for tax depreciation allowance of $40,000 in the year ended 31 December 20X8.

JW has an under-provision on the tax account bought forward for the year for $3,950, representing an under-payment for the year ended 31 December 20X7.

42   **Calculate the corporate income tax payable by JW for the year ended 31 December 20X8.**

$ _____ . (Your answer should be rounded down to the nearest $.)

43   **Calculate income tax expense to be shown on JW's statement of profit or loss for the year ended 31 December 20X8.**

$ _____ . (Your answer should be rounded down to the nearest $.)

Data for Questions 44 and 45

The following is an extract from KM's statement of profit or loss for the year ended 31 March 20X1:

	$
Revenue	966,000
Cost of sales	(520,000)
Gross profit	446,000
Administrative expenses	(174,000)
Distribution costs	(40,000)
	232,000
Finance cost	(67,000)
Profit before tax	165,000

Cost of sales includes depreciation charges of $42,000 for property, plant and equipment. Distribution costs include a depreciation charge for a new vehicle (see below). Included in administrative expenses are entertainment costs of $9,800. These expenses are to be treated as disallowable for the year.

KM had been selling through retail outlets, but from 1 April 20X0 began selling on the internet and delivering to customers as well. KM purchased its first delivery vehicle on 1 April 20X0 for $18,000. The vehicle qualifies for a first year tax allowance of 50% and is depreciated on a straight line basis over six years.

The property, plant and equipment (excluding the delivery vehicle) qualified for tax depreciation allowance of $65,000 in the year ended 31 March 20X1.

Taxation is to be charged at 25%.

KM has an over-provision on the tax account bought forward for the year for $7,250, representing an over-payment for the year ended 31 March 20X1.

44 Calculate the corporate income tax payable by KM for the year ended 31 March 20X1.

$ _____. (Your answer should be rounded down to the nearest $.)

45 Calculate income tax expense to be shown on KM's statement of profit or loss for the year ended 31 March 20X1.

$ _____. (Your answer should be rounded down to the nearest $.)

46 HG is resident in Country X.

HG had a tax loss of $49,000 for the year ended 31 December 20X1.

HG made an accounting profit of $167,000 for the year ended 31 December 20X2. The profit was after charging $4,000 for entertaining and $5,000 for donations to a political party. HG's revenue includes a non-taxable government grant of $12,000 received during the year ended 31 December 20X2.

HG has plant and equipment that cost $50,000 on 1 January 20X1 and new equipment that cost $8,000 on 1 January 20X2. HG depreciates its plant and equipment on a straight line basis over 5 years with no residual value.

All expenses other than depreciation, amortisation, entertaining, taxes paid to other public bodies and donations to political parties are tax deductible.

Tax depreciation is deductible as follows:

- 50% of additions to property, plant and equipment in the accounting period in which they are recorded

- 25% per year of the written-down value (i.e. cost minus previous allowances) in subsequent accounting periods except that in which the asset is disposed of.

The corporate tax on profits is at a rate of 25%.

Calculate the tax payable by HG for the year ended 31 December 20X2.

$ _____. (Your answer should be rounded down to the nearest $.)

47 Governments use a range of specific excise duties as well as general sales taxes on goods.

Which of following don NOT explain a reason why a government might apply a specific excise duty to a category of goods?

A   It may want to raise extra revenue from luxury products that people will buy regardless of cost

B   To discourage use of harmful substances by making them expensive to buy, i.e. tobacco and alcohol

C   To pay for the healthcare that harmful substances cause, i.e. medical treatment from smokers

D   It may want to raise extra revenue from elastic products

48   **Place the following options into the highlighted boxes in the table below to correctly show the difference between a single stage and a multi-stage sales tax. The options cannot be used more than once.**

| Tax at one level of production |
| This could be VAT |
| This could be cascade tax |
| Tax at each level of production |
| Single stage |
| Multi-stage |

Type of tax		
Characteristic		
Characteristic		
Characteristic		

49   WX is a business in Country X that uses locally grown fruit and vegetables to make country wines. During 20X9 W paid $30,000 plus VAT for the ingredients and other running costs.

When the wine is bottled W pays $1 tax per bottle to the tax authority. During 20X9 W produced 10,000 bottles.

W sold all the wine to retailers for an average of $8.05 per bottle, including VAT at standard rate of 15%.

Place the following options into the highlighted boxes in the table below to correctly show the difference between a unit tax and an ad valorem tax. The options cannot be used more than once.

| This is charged on weight or size |
| This is charged on the value of the units sold |
| Example WZ sells for $8.05 inclusive of VAT at 15% |
| Example WZ pays $1 per bottle sold |
| Unit tax |
| Ad valorem tax |

Type of tax		
Characteristic		
Characteristic		

50   Once registered for VAT an entity must abide by the VAT regulations.

Which THREE of the following are typical requirements of VAT regulations?

A   Complete a quarterly VAT return

B   Charge VAT on all supplies to customers

C   Keep appropriate VAT records

D   Make payments to VAT authority and be able to claim back VAT when due

E   Recover VAT on all purchases from suppliers

F   Complete a monthly VAT return

51   Trading losses in any period can be carried back and set off against profits in the previous 12-month period, and any unrelieved losses should be carried forward to set against profits in future years. Trading losses cannot be set off against capital gains. Capital losses should be set off against capital gains in the same tax year, but unrelieved capital losses cannot be carried back. Unrelieved capital losses should be carried forward and set against capital gains in future years.

QWE had the following taxable profits, gains and losses in years 1 to 4.

	Trading profits/(losses)	Capital gains/(losses)
	$	$
Year 1	50,000	6,000
Year 2	(90,000)	(8,000)
Year 3	30,000	5,000
Year 4	70,000	6,000

Place the following options into the highlighted boxes in the table below to correctly reflect QWE's taxable profits and gains in each year. The options can be used more than once and not all options have to be used.

$ nil
$3,000
$6,000
$10,000
$60,000

Year	Taxable profits	Taxable gains
1		
2		
3		
4		

52   What is the nature of group loss relief?

A   Profits and losses of all companies in the same group are consolidated and taxed at the same rate

B   Losses of subsidiaries must be set off against the profits of the parent company in the group

C   Members of the group may surrender their losses to any other member of the group

D   Companies in the same group are required by the tax authorities to surrender their losses to any other subsidiary in the group

53   Country B has a corporate income tax system that treats capital gains/losses separately from trading profits/losses. Capital gains/losses cannot be offset against trading profits/losses. All losses can be carried forward indefinitely, but cannot be carried back to previous years. Trading profits and capital gains are both taxed at 20%.

BD had no brought forward losses on 1 October 20X2. BD's results for 20X3 to 20X5 were as follows:

	Trading profit/(loss)	Capital gains/(loss)
	$000	$000
Year to September 20X3	200	(100)
Year to September 20X4	(120)	0
Year to September 20X5	150	130

Place the following options into the highlighted boxes in the table below to correctly reflect BD's corporate income tax and capital tax due for each of the years ended 30 September 20X3 to 20X5. The options can be used more than once and not all options have to be used.

$ nil	$6,000
$14,000	$30,000
$16,000	$70,000
$40,000	$80,000

Year	Corporate income tax due	Capital tax due
30 September 20X3		
30 September 20X4		
30 September 20X5		

54   **Which TWO of the following statements are reasons why a group of entities might want to claim group loss relief rather than use the loss in the entity to which it relates?**

A   Relief can be claimed as earlier because the surrendering entity does not expect to make a profit in the foreseeable future

B   Tax can be saved because the entity the loss is surrendered to pays a lower rate of tax than the surrendering entity

C   The surrendering entity will receive a tax refund for their loss if it is surrendered to another group entity

D   Tax can be saved because the entity the loss is surrendered to pays a higher rate of tax than the surrendering entity

E   The entity receiving the loss will receive a tax refund for the loss

55 BCF purchased an asset for $600,000 on 1 September 20X4. BCF incurred additional purchase costs of $5,000.

Indexation of the cost of BCF's asset is allowed in Country X. The relevant index increased by 60% in the period from 1 September 20X4 to 31 August 20Y1.

BCF sold the asset on 1 September 20Y1 for $1,200,000. BCF incurred selling costs of $9,000.

Assume all purchase and selling costs are tax allowable.

Tax is charged at 25%.

How much tax was due from BCF on disposal of its asset?

A $55,750

B $56,500

C $64,250

D $146,500

56 EG purchased a property for $630,000 on 1 September 20X0. EG incurred additional costs for the purchase of $3,500 surveyors' fees and $6,500 legal fees. EG then spent $100,000 renovating the property prior to letting it. All of EG's expenditure was classified as capital expenditure according to the local tax regulations.

Indexation of the purchase and renovation costs is allowed on EE's property. The index increased by 50% between September 20X0 and October 20X7. Assume that acquisition and renovation costs were incurred in September 20X0. EG sold the property on 1 October 20X7 for $1,250,000, incurring tax allowable costs on disposal of $2,000.

Calculate EG's tax due on disposal assuming a tax rate of 30%.

$ _____. (Your answer should be rounded down to the nearest $.)

57 CG purchased an asset on 1 April 20X6 for $650,000, exclusive of import duties of $25,000. CG is resident in Country X where the indexation factor increased by 50% in the period from 1 April 20X6 to 31 March 20Y3.

CG sold the asset on 31 March 20Y3 for $1,200,000 incurring transaction charges of $17,000.

Capital gains are taxed at 25%.

Calculate the capital gains tax due from CG on disposal of the asset.

$ _____. (Your answer should be rounded down to the nearest $.)

58 RS purchased an asset on 1 April 20X0 for $375,000, incurring legal fees of $12,000. RS is resident in Country X. There was no indexation allowed on the asset.

RS sold the asset on 31 March 20X3 for $450,000 incurring transaction charges of $15,000.

Tax is charged at 25%.

Calculate the capital gains tax due from RS on disposal of the asset.

$ _____. (Your answer should be rounded down to the nearest $.)

59   The OECD Model tax convention defines a permanent establishment.

Which of the following is NOT specifically listed as a permanent establishment by the OECD Model tax convention?

A   An office

B   A factory

C   An oil well

D   A site of an 11 month construction project

60   Where a resident entity runs an overseas operation as a branch of the entity, certain tax implications arise.

Which of the following does NOT usually apply in relation to an overseas branch?

A   Assets can be transferred to the branch without triggering a capital gain

B   Corporate income tax is paid on profits remitted by the branch

C   Tax depreciation can be claimed on any qualifying assets used in the trade of the branch

D   Losses sustained by the branch are immediately deductible against the resident entity's income

61   **A withholding tax is:**

A   tax withheld from payment to the tax authorities

B   tax paid less an amount withheld from payment

C   tax deducted at source before payment of interest or dividends

D   tax paid on increases in value of investment holdings

62   **Place the following options into the highlighted boxes in the table below to correctly show the difference between cascade sales tax and value added tax (VAT). The options can be used more than once and not all options have to be used.**

| No refunds are provided by local government on purchase tax |
| Refunds are provided on purchase tax provided the purchases are used for a taxable supply |
| Tax at one level of production |
| Tax at each level of production |
| Single stage |
| Multi-stage |

Type of tax	Cascade tax	VAT
Characteristic		
Characteristic		
Characteristic		

63   JK, an entity operating in Country X, purchased land on 1 March 20X6 for $850,000. JK incurred purchase costs of surveyor's fees $5,000 and legal fees $8,000. JK spent $15,000 clearing the land and making it suitable for development. Local tax regulations classified all of JK's expenditure as capital expenditure.

JK sold the land for $1,000,000 on 1 February 20X9, incurring tax allowable costs of $6,000.

Tax is charged at a rate of 25%.

No indexation is allowable on the sale of land.

Calculate the capital tax payable by JK on the disposal of the land.

$ _____. (Your answer should be rounded down to the nearest $.)

64   **Complete the sentence below by placing one of the following options in the space.**

The Organisation of Economic Co-operation and Development's (OECD) model tax convention defines corporate residence.

Under the OECD model an entity will have residence in _____.

the country of incorporation
the country where the directors reside
the country of effective management
the country where most production arises

65   Corporate residence for tax purposes can be determined in a number of ways, depending on the country concerned.

Which of the following is NOT normally used to determine corporate residence for tax purposes?

A   The country from which control of the entity is exercised

B   The country of incorporation of the entity

C   The country where the management of the entity holds its meetings

D   The country where most of the entity's products are sold

66   The following details relate to EA:

- it was incorporated in Country A

- it carries out its main business activities in Country B

- its senior management operate from Country C and effective control is exercised from Country C.

Assume countries A, B and C have all signed double tax treaties with each other, based on the OECD model tax convention.

In which country will EA be deemed to be resident for tax purposes?

A   Country A

B   Country B

C   Country C

D   Both Countries B and C

67 EB has an investment of 25% of the equity shares in XY, an entity resident in a foreign country.

EB receives a dividend of $90,000 from XY, the amount being after the deduction of tax amounting to $10,000 deducted at source in the foreign country.

The $10,000 can be explained as what type of tax?

A   Corporate tax

B   Underlying tax

C   Capital tax

D   Withholding tax

68 **Double tax relief is used to:**

A   ensure that you do not pay tax twice on any of your income

B   mitigate taxing overseas income twice

C   avoid taxing dividends received from subsidiaries in the same country twice

D   provide relief where a company pays tax at double the normal rate

69 The following details are relevant:

- HC carries out its main business activities in Country A

- HC is incorporated in Country B

- HC's senior management exercise control from Country C, but there are no sales or purchases made in Country C

- HC raises its finance and is quoted on the stock exchange in Country D

Assume Countries A, B, C and D have all signed double taxation treaties with each other, based on the OECD model tax convention.

Which country will HC be deemed to be resident in for tax purposes?

A   Country A

B   Country B

C   Country C

D   Country D

70 AB made a profit of $320,000 for the year ended 31 December 20X2 and paid $80,000 tax on its profits. AB pays a gross dividend of $150,000 to its holding company, which operates in a foreign country. When AB pays the dividend it deducts a 10% tax.

This 10% tax is called:

A   underlying tax

B   corporate income tax

C   foreign tax

D   withholding tax

71 Which TWO of the following are methods of giving double taxation relief?

A Tax credit relief

B Deduction relief

C Tax loss relief

D Withholding relief

E Underlying relief

72 Which of the following gives the meaning of rollover relief?

A Trading losses can be carried forward to future years

B Inventory can be valued using current values instead of original cost

C Capital losses made in a period can be carried forward to future years

D Payment of tax on a capital gain can be delayed if the full proceeds from the sale of an asset are reinvested in a replacement asset

73 MT's summarised statement of profit or loss for the year ended 31 March 20X3 is as follows:

	$
Gross profit	187,000
Administrative expenses	(126,000)
Distribution costs	(22,000)
	39,000
Finance cost	(2,000)
Profit before tax	37,000

Administrative expenses include donations to the local ruling political party of $5,000 and depreciation of property, plant and equipment of $39,000 (inclusive of depreciation of new purchases).

MT an entity operating in Country X made a tax loss for the year ended 31 March 20X2. The loss carried forward at 31 March 20X2 was $12,000.

At 31 March 20X2 MT's tax written down value of its property, plant and equipment was $120,000. All of these assets qualified for the annual tax depreciation allowances. MT purchased property, plant and equipment during the year to 31 March 20X3 for $30,000.

All expenses other than depreciation, amortisation, entertaining, taxes paid to other public bodies and donations to political parties are tax deductible.

Tax depreciation is deductible as follows:

- 50% of additions to property, plant and equipment in the accounting period in which they are recorded

- 25% per year of the written-down value (i.e. cost minus previous allowances) in subsequent accounting periods except that in which the asset is disposed of

- Tax losses can be carried forward to offset against future taxable profits from the same business.

Place the following options into the highlighted boxes in the table below to correctly reflect MT's taxable profit for the year ended 31 March 20X3. The options cannot be used more than once and not all options have to be used.

Donations	$5,000	($5,000)
Accounting depreciation	$39,000	($39,000)
Tax depreciation	$45,000	($45,000)
$24,000	$48,000	($12,000)
$12,000	$50,000	$26,000

MT – Corporate income tax	$
Accounting profit	37,000
Tax losses	
	———
Taxable profit	

74 Place the following options into the highlighted boxes in the table below to correctly the difference between exempt and zero rated supplies. The options cannot be used more than once.

Entity must register for VAT purposes
Entity does not register for VAT purposes
VAT can be claimed back on purchases
VAT cannot be claimed back on purchases

Type of supply	Zero rated	Exempt
Characteristic		
Characteristic		

75 Complete the sentence below by placing one of the following options in the space.

A capital gain is _____.

the trading profit of an entity transferred to equity
the profit made on the disposal of a chargeable asset
the taxable profit of an entity

76 Complete the sentence below by placing one of the following options in the space.

Capital tax is _____.

the tax charged on the trading profit of an entity before it is transferred to equity
the tax charged on the profit made on the disposal of a chargeable asset
the tax charged on the taxable profit of an entity

77   On 31 March 20X6, CH had a credit balance brought forward on its corporate income tax account of $31,000, representing an over-provision of the tax charge for the year ended 31 March 20X5.

CH's taxable profit for the year ended 31 March 20X6 was $946,000 and the applicable income tax rate for the year to 31 March 20X6 as 22%.

Calculate the income tax expense that CH will charge in its statement of profit or loss for the year ended 31 March 20X6, as required by IAS 12 Income Taxes.

$ _____. (Your answer should be rounded down to the nearest $.)

78   DZ recognised a tax liability of $290,000 in its financial statements for the year ended 30 September 20X5. This was subsequently agreed with and paid to the tax authorities as $280,000 on 1 March 20X6. The directors of DZ estimate that the tax due on the profits for the year to 30 September 20X6 will be $320,000.

What is DZ's statement of profit or loss tax charge for the year ended 30 September 20X6?

A $310,000

B $320,000

C $330,000

D $600,000

79   **Complete the sentence below by placing one of the following options in the space.**

A tax base represents _____.

| the tax written down value of an asset |
| what is being taxed |
| the taxable profit of an entity |

80   The tax year runs from 1 May to 30 April. An individual's accounting year ends on 31 December. AB's taxable profits for the year to 31 December 20X4 were $75,000.

The rate of tax chargeable on AB's profits is as follows:

| Year to 30 April 20X4 | 20% |
| Year to 30 April 20X5 | 25% |

On the basis of this information, calculate the tax payable for the year to 31 December 20X4.

$ _____. (Your answer should be rounded down to the nearest $.)

81   **Which THREE of following are examples of the different tax bases regularly used by governments?**

A   Income

B   Equity

C   Capital

D   Benefits

E   Consumption

F   Losses

82   EF has an accounting profit before tax of $95,000. The tax rate on trading profits applicable to EF for the year is 25%. The accounting profit included non-taxable income from government grants of $15,000 and non-tax allowable expenditure of $10,000 on entertaining expenses.

Calculate the tax payable by EF for the year.

$ _____. (Your answer should be rounded down to the nearest $.)

83   **Complete the sentence below by placing one of the following options in the space.**

Benefits in kind represent _____.

all benefits given to an employee as part of their remuneration package
cash benefits given to an employee as part of their remuneration package
non-cash benefits given to an employee as part of their remuneration package

84   For the year ended 30 September 20X2 KQ's income statement included a profit before tax of $147,000. KQ's expenses included political donations of $9,000 and entertaining expenses of $6,000.

KQ's statement of financial position at 30 September 20X2 included plant and machinery with a carrying value of $168,500. This is comprised of plant purchased on 1 October 20X0 at a cost of $180,000 and machinery purchased on 1 October 20X1 at a cost of $50,000.

KQ depreciates all plant and machinery on the straight line basis at 15% per year.

All expenses other than depreciation, amortisation, entertaining, taxes paid to other public bodies and donations to political parties are tax deductible.

Tax depreciation is deductible as follows:

- 50% of additions to property, plant and equipment in the accounting period in which they are recorded

- 25% per year of the written-down value (i.e. cost minus previous allowances) in subsequent accounting periods except that in which the asset is disposed of.

The corporate tax on profits is at a rate of 25%.

Calculate the tax payable by KQ for the year to 30 September 20X2.

$ _____. (Your answer should be rounded down to the nearest $.)

85   **Which THREE of the following statements are true regarding excise duties?**

A   Suitable for inelastic products

B   They are a unit tax

C   Suitable for elastic products

D   Suitable when there are few producers

E   They are an ad valorem tax

F   Suitable when there are many producers

86 EE reported accounting profits of $822,000 for the period ended 30 November 20X7. This was after deducting entertaining expenses of $32,000 and a donation to a political party of $50,000, both of which are disallowable for tax purposes.

EE's reported profit also included $103,000 government grant income that was exempt from taxation. EE paid dividends of $240,000 in the period.

Assume the tax rate is 25%.

Calculate EE's tax payable be on its profits for the year to 30 November 20X7.

$ _____. (Your answer should be rounded down to the nearest $.)

87 **Place the following options into the highlighted boxes in the table below to correctly the difference between tax avoidance and tax evasion. The options cannot be used more than once.**

| An illegal way of reducing your tax bill |
| A legal way of reducing your tax bill |
| For example AB does not declare his income from his night security job |
| For example AB invests surplus income into tax-free securities to avoid paying tax on the interest |

	Tax avoidance	Tax evasion
Characteristic		
Characteristic		

88 **An underlying tax is:**

A   the tax deducted at source from the foreign income before it is distributed

B   the tax on the profits out of which a dividend is paid

C   the amount of tax relief that can be claimed for double tax relief purposes

D   the tax paid in the country of residency on foreign income

89 **Which TWO of the following are statutory powers that a tax authority may be granted to ensure compliance with tax regulations?**

(i)   Power to arrest individuals

(ii)   Power of entry and search of premises

(iii) Power to exchange information with other tax authorities

(v)   Power to confiscate assets of the entity

A   (i) and (iii)

B   (i) and (iv)

C   (ii) and (iii)

D   (ii) and (iv)

90 **Which of the following is the correct meaning of rollover relief?**

A   A trading loss can be carried forward and used to reduce tax in a future profitable year

B   A capital loss incurred on the disposal of an asset can be carried forward to a future tax year

C   An entity ceasing to trade, carrying back a trading loss to set off against previous years' profits

D   A gain arising from the sale of an asset is deferred provided the entity reinvests the proceeds of the sale in a replacement asset

91 SB operates in Country X and is considering starting business activities in a foreign country.

An entity may conduct a foreign operation through a branch or a subsidiary.

Which of the following is an advantage of SB operating its foreign operation as a subsidiary?

A   A loss made by the foreign operation will be available to the SB group

B   SB will only pay tax on dividends received from its foreign operation

C   All profits/losses overseas will be subject to tax in Country X

D   SB can claim tax depreciation on its foreign operation's assets

92 The government of Country X has estimated the following for the year ended 31 December 20X4:

- Total income tax due $166 billion

- Total income tax expected to be collected $135 billion

- Income tax that will not be collected due to tax evasion $10 billion

- Income tax that will not be collected due to tax avoidance $15 billion

The tax gap for the year to 31 December 20X4 is expected to be:

A $6 billion

B $16 billion

C $21 billion

D $31 billion

93 AB, incorporated in Country X, purchased a non-depreciable asset for $55,000 on 1 January 20X2. AB incurred additional purchase costs of $5,000.

The asset was eventually sold for $210,000 on 31 December 20X5.

The indexation factor from 1 January 20X2 to 31 December 20X5 was 15%.

Tax is charged at 25% on gains.

Calculate the capital tax payable by AB on the disposal of the asset.

$ _____. (Your answer should be rounded down to the nearest $.)

94 **Which of the following is regarded as a direct tax?**

A   Value added tax

B   Capital gains tax

C   Excise duties

D   Property tax

95 UI has the following details:

(i)   Incorporated in Country A.

(ii)   Senior management hold regular board meetings in Country B and exercise control from there, but there are no sales or purchases made in Country B.

(iii)   Carries out its main business activities in Country C.

Assume all three countries have double taxation treaties with each other, based on the OECD model tax convention.

In which country/countries will UI be deemed to be resident for tax purposes?

A   Country A

B   Country B

C   Country C

D   Countries B and C

96 UV purchased an asset for $50,000 on 1 October 20X6, incurring import duties of $8,000. UV depreciated the asset at 10% per year on a straight line basis.

UV sold the asset for $80,000 on 30 September 20X9, incurring costs of $2,000. The asset was subject to capital gains tax of 25% and the indexation factor from 1 October 20X6 to 30 September 20X9 was 14%.

Calculate the capital tax payable by UV on the disposal of the asset.

$ _____. (Your answer should be rounded down to the nearest $.)

97 YZ, incorporated in Country X, purchased a non-depreciable asset for $45,000 on 1 January 20X1. YZ incurred additional purchase costs of $5,000.

The asset was eventually sold for $110,000 on 31 December 20X3.

The indexation factor from 1 January 20X1 to 31 December 20X3 was 35%.

Tax is charged on gains at 25%.

Calculate the capital tax payable by YZ on the disposal of the asset.

A $10,625

B $16,250

C $42,500

D $60,000

98 **Complete the sentence below by placing one of the following options in the space.**

An indexation allowance _____.

| increases a chargeable gain |
| reduces a chargeable gain |
| increases a taxable profit |
| reduces a taxable profit |

99 In Country Y, A earns $75,000 profit for the year and receives a tax bill for $15,000.

B earns $40,000 profit for the year and receives a tax bill for $8,000.

Country Y's income tax could be said to be a:

A   Regressive tax

B   Proportional tax

C   Progressive tax

D   Fixed rate tax

100 **Place TWO of the following options into the highlighted boxes in the table below to correctly explain the characteristics of transfer pricing.**

| This results in transactions not taking place at 'arm's length' and profits being effected by the group members |
| This does not have an effect on individual entity profits for tax purposes |
| This arises in group situations when either goods are sold inter-company or a loans take place at a favourable price |
| This effect the calculation of the group profit for tax purposes |

	Transfer pricing
Characteristic	
Characteristic	

REGULATORY ENVIRONMENT FOR FINANCIAL REPORTING AND CORPORATE GOVERNANCE

101 The IASB's The Conceptual Framework for Financial Reporting defines elements of financial statements.

Complete the sentence below by placing one of the following options in the space.

An asset is a _____.

| resource controlled by the entity as a result of past events and from which future economic benefits are expected to flow to the entity |
| resource controlled by the entity as a result of past events and from which future economic benefits are expected to flow from the entity |

102 In connection with the role of the external auditor, which of the following statements are TRUE?

(i) The auditor certifies that the financial statements of an entity give a true and fair view.

(ii) It is not a primary duty of the auditor to seek out fraud.

(iii) The directors, not the auditor have the primary responsibility for the preparation of annual financial statements and the setting up of a suitable internal control system.

(iv) The auditor has the right of access at all times to the books, records, documents and accounts of the company.

A All four statements

B (ii), (iii) and (iv) only

C (iii) and (iv) only

D (iv) only

103 When an external auditor is unable to agree the accounting treatment of a material item with the directors of an entity, but the financial statements are not seriously misleading, he will issue:

A an unmodified audit report

B an adverse opinion

C a modified audit report using 'except for'

D an unmodified audit report using 'except for'

104 According to the IASB's The Conceptual Framework for Financial Reporting, what is the objective of financial statements?

Complete the sentence below by placing one of the following options in the space.

The objective of financial reporting is _____.

to prepare ledger accounts for every transaction to enable financial statements to be prepared
to provide information about the reporting entity that is useful to a wide range of users in making economic decisions
to record transactions for in order to produce a trial balance and financial statements
to present the results so that management can make economic decisions and decide how to allocate resources

105 Financial statements prepared using International Standards and the International Accounting Standards Board's (IASB) The Conceptual Framework for Financial Reporting are presumed to apply one of the following four underlying assumptions.

Which of the following is an underlying assumption according to the IASB's Framework?

A Relevance

B Going concern

C Prudence

D Accruals

106 **What is the main function of the IFRS Interpretations Committee?**

    A   Issuing International Financial Reporting Standards

    B   Withdrawing International Financial Reporting Standards

    C   Overseeing the development of International Financial Reporting Standards

    D   Interpreting the application of International Financial Reporting Standards

107 **In the organisation structure for the regulation and supervision of International Accounting Standards, which of the bodies listed below acts as the overall supervisory body?**

    A   IFRS Foundation

    B   International Accounting Standards Board

    C   IFRS Advisory Council

    D   IFRS Interpretations Committee

108 An auditor disagrees with the accounting treatment adopted by a company. The impact of the item concerned is seen to be material, but not pervasive.

    Which TWO of the following types of audit report and opinion would be appropriate?

    A   Unmodified report

    B   Modified report

    C   Disclaimer of opinion

    D   Adverse opinion

    E   Qualified opinion

109 An external auditor gives a modified audit report that is a disclaimer of opinion.

    This means that the auditor:

    A   has been unable to agree with an accounting treatment used by the directors in relation to a material item

    B   has been prevented from obtaining sufficient appropriate audit evidence

    C   has found extensive errors in the financial statements and concludes that they do not show a true and fair view

    D   has discovered a few immaterial differences that do not affect the auditor's opinion

110 An external auditor has completed an audit and is satisfied that proper records have been maintained and that the financial statements reflect those transactions. However the auditor has one disagreement with the management of the entity. The disagreement involves the treatment of one large item of expenditure that has been classified by management as an increase in non-current assets. The auditor is of the opinion that the item should have been classified as maintenance and charged as an expense to the statement of profit or loss and other comprehensive income. The amount is material in the context of the reported profit for the year.

Assuming that the management refuse to change their approach, which of the following modified audit reports should the auditor use?

A   Emphasis of matter

B   Qualified opinion

C   Adverse opinion

D   Disclaimer of opinion

111 The external auditor has a duty to report on the truth and fairness of the financial statements and to report any reservations. The auditor is normally given a number of powers by statute to enable the statutory duties to be carried out.

Place THREE of the following options into the highlighted boxes in the table below to correctly explain the powers that are usually granted to the auditor by statute.

Power to access the books, records, documents and accounts
Power to change financial statements when disagreements are found
Power to attend and speak at meetings of equity holders
Power to require officers of the entity to provide them with information and explanations
Power to share information with international tax bodies

Powers of auditors

112 **Which TWO of the following is NOT a topic included in the International Accounting Standards Board's (IASB) The Conceptual Framework for Financial Reporting?**

A   The objective of financial statements

B   Concepts of capital maintenance

C   Regulatory bodies governing financial statements

D   Measurement of the elements of financial statements

E   The standard setting process

113 The IASB's The Conceptual Framework for Financial Reporting defines five elements of financial statements.

Complete the sentence below by placing one of the following options in the two spaces.

The elements are assets, liabilities, income, _____ and _____.

expenses	equity
capital	expenditure
losses	profit

114 **Which of the powers listed below is unlikely to be granted to the auditor by legislation?**

A The right of access at all times to the books, records, documents and accounts of the entity

B The right to be notified of, attend, and speak at meetings of equity holders

C The right to correct financial statements if the auditor believes the statements do not show a true and fair view

D The right to require officers of the entity to provide whatever information and explanations thought necessary for the performance of the duties of the auditor

115 **Which of the following statements would be TRUE when an independent auditor's report gives an adverse opinion?**

A The effect of the disagreement with management is so pervasive that the financial statements are misleading and, in the opinion of the auditor, do not give a true and fair view

B A disagreement with management over material items needs to be highlighted using an 'except for' statement

C An opinion cannot be given because insufficient information or access to records has been given to the auditor

D A disagreement with management over material items means that an unmodified report must be issued

116 **Which THREE of the following are functions of the IFRS Committee Foundation?**

A Issuing International Accounting Standards

B Approving the annual budget of the IASB and its committees

C Enforcing International Accounting Standards

D Reviewing the strategy of the IASB

E Publishing an annual report on the activities of the IASB

F Interpreting International Accounting Standards

117 The external auditors have completed the audit of GQ for the year ended 30 June 20X8 and have several outstanding differences of opinion that they have been unable to resolve with the management of GQ. The senior partner of the external auditors has reviewed these outstanding differences and concluded that individually and in aggregate the differences are not material.

Which of the following audit opinions will the external auditors use for GQ's financial statements for the year ended 30 June 20X8?

A   An unmodified opinion

B   An adverse opinion

C   An emphasis of matter

D   A qualified opinion

118 **Complete the sentence below by placing one of the following options into each of the two spaces.**

The IASB's Framework identifies two methods of capital maintenance which are the _____ concept and the _____ concept.

physical	accruals
going concern	financial
prudence	consistency

119 **Complete the sentence below by placing one of the following options into the space.**

The IASB's Framework identifies the underlying assumption as the_____ concept.

matching	accruals
going concern	faithful representation
prudence	consistency

120 **Place TWO of the following options into the highlighted boxes in the table below to correctly explain the objective of an external audit.**

To see if the financial statements are correct with no errors
To see if the financial statements show a true and fair view
To correct the financial statements if any errors are discovered
To see if the financial statements have been prepared in accordance with appropriate accounting standards

The objective of an external audit

121 **Which of the following gives the best description of the objectives of financial statements as set out by the IASB's The Conceptual Framework for Financial Reporting?**

    A   To fairly present the financial position and performance of an entity

    B   To fairly present the financial position, performance and changes in financial position of an entity

    C   To provide information about the financial position and performance of an entity that is useful to a wide range of users in making economic decisions

    D   To provide information about the financial position, performance and changes in financial position of an entity that is useful to a wide range of users in making economic decisions

122 **The IASB's The Conceptual Framework for Financial Reporting defines a liability as:**

    A   an amount owed to another entity

    B   a present obligation arising as a result of past events, the settlement of which is expected to result in an outflow of economic benefits

    C   expenditure that has been incurred but not yet charged to the statement of profit or loss

    D   an obligation that may arise in the future

123 **Under the IASB's The Conceptual Framework for Financial Reporting the threshold quality of useful financial information is:**

    A   relevance

    B   reliability

    C   materiality

    D   understandability

124 The IASB's The Conceptual Framework for Financial Reporting provides definitions of the elements of financial statements. One of the elements defined by the Framework is expenses.

Complete the sentence below by placing one of the following options in the space.

Expenses are _____.

decreases in economic benefits during the accounting period in the form of outflows or depletions of assets or incurrence's of liabilities that result in decreases in equity, other than those relating to distributions to equity participants
increases in economic benefits during the accounting period in the form of outflows or depletions of assets or incurrence's of liabilities that result in increases in equity, other than those relating to distributions to equity participants

125 **Which of the following is NOT a function of the IASB?**

A   Enforcing international financial reporting standards

B   Issuing international financial reporting standards

C   Approving International Financial Reporting Interpretations Committee's interpretations of international financial reporting standards

D   Issuing exposure drafts for public comment

126 **The IASB's The Conceptual Framework for Financial Reporting is the IASB's conceptual framework. Which TWO of the following does the Framework NOT cover?**

A   The format of financial statements

B   The objective of financial statements

C   Concepts of capital maintenance

D   The elements of financial statements

E   The users of the financial statements

127 **According to the IASB's The Conceptual Framework for Financial Reporting, equity is described as:**

A   the amount paid into the enterprise by the owner

B   accumulated profits less amounts withdrawn

C   the residual interest in the assets less liabilities

D   owner's capital investment in the enterprise

128 The IASB's The Conceptual Framework for Financial Reporting lists two fundamental qualitative characteristics of financial statements, one of which is faithful representation.

Which of the following is NOT a characteristic of faithful representation?

A   Completeness

B   Neutrality

C   Free from error

D   Prudence

129 An external auditor gives a modified audit report that is a disclaimer of opinion.

This means that the auditor has:

A   been unable to access sufficient appropriate audit evidence

B   been unable to agree with the directors over an accounting treatment of a material item

C   found a few immaterial errors that have no impact on the auditor's opinion

D   found many errors causing material misstatements and has concluded that the financial statements do not present fairly the financial position and financial performance

130 E, a trainee management accountant, prepares an annual analysis of the performance of all staff, including her own. The analysis is used by the financial director to calculate staff bonuses each year.

According to the CIMA code of ethics for professional accountants which of the threats listed below would apply to E?

- A Advocacy threat
- B Intimidation threat
- C Familiarity threat
- D Self-interest threat

131 Accounting and information disclosure practices are influenced by a variety of factors around the world.

Place THREE of the following options into the highlighted boxes in the table below to correctly identify these factors.

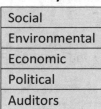

| Social |
| Environmental |
| Economic |
| Political |
| Auditors |

Factors influencing accounting and disclosure

132 **Which of the following is a function of the IFRS Foundation?**

- A Complete responsibility for the preparation and publication of International Financial Reporting Standards (IFRSs)
- B Approving annually the budget and determining the funding of the International Accounting Standards Board (IASB)
- C To inform the IASB of the views of organisations and individuals on major standard setting projects
- D To review new financial reporting issues not yet covered by an IFRS

133 An external auditor gives a modified audit report that is an adverse opinion.

This means that the auditor:

- A has been unable to agree with the directors over an accounting treatment of a material but not pervasive item
- B has been unable to access important accounting records
- C was unable to attend the inventory count and is unable to agree the inventory value, which is material
- D has found many errors causing material misstatements in the financial statements

134 R, a trainee management accountant is employed by JH. R has prepared the draft annual financial statements for JH and presented them to JH's Chief Executive prior to the executive board meeting. The Chief Executive has told R that the profit reported in the financial statements is too low and must be increased by $500,000 before the financial statements can be approved by the executive board.

Which of the threats listed below would apply to R in this situation, according to the CIMA code of ethics for professional accountants?

A   Advocacy threat

B   Self-review threat

C   Intimidation threat

D   Self-interest threat

135 **Place THREE of the following options into the highlighted boxes in the table below to correctly explain the functions of the IFRS Advisory Council.**

Approving annually the budget and determining the funding of the IASB
To give advice to the IASB on agenda decisions
Review, on a timely basis, new financial reporting issues not specifically addressed in IFRSs
To give advice to the IASB on the priorities in its work
To give any other advice to the IASB or the Trustees
Reviewing annually the strategy of the IASB and its effectiveness

Functions of the IFRS Advisory Council

136 **Complete the sentence below by placing one of the following options into each of the two spaces.**

The IASB's The Conceptual Framework for Financial Reporting splits qualitative characteristics of useful information into two categories, fundamental and enhancing.

The TWO fundamental qualitative characteristics are _____ and _____.

comparability	faithful representation
relevance	neutral
materiality	understandability

137   An external audit report usually has the following 5 sections:

(i)   Title and addressee

(ii)   Introduction

(iii)   Scope

(iv)   ***

(v)   Signature and name of audit firm

Complete the sentence below by placing one of the following options into the space.

Item (iv) of the report is _____.

| Opinion |
| Conclusion |
| Outcome |

138   The following are possible methods of measuring assets and liabilities other than historical cost:

(i)   Current cost

(ii)   Realisable value

(iii)   Present value

(iv)   Replacement cost

According to the IASB's The Conceptual Framework for Financial Reporting which of the measurement bases above can be used by an entity for measuring assets and liabilities shown in its statement of financial position?

A   (i) and (ii)

B   (i), (ii) and (iii)

C   (ii) and (iii)

D   (i), (ii) (iii) and (iv)

139   **Which of the following bodies is responsible for the approval of interpretations of international financial reporting standards before they are issued?**

A   IASB

B   IFRS Advisory Council

C   IFRS Foundation

D   IFRS Interpretations Committee

140   The IASB's The Conceptual Framework for Financial Reporting identifies qualitative characteristics of financial statements.

Characteristics

(i)   Relevance

(ii)   Reliability

(iii)   Faithful representation

(iv)   Comparability

Which of the above characteristics are NOT fundamental qualitative characteristics according to the IASB's Framework?

A   (i) and (ii)

B   (i) and (iii)

C   (iii) and (iv)

D   (ii) and (iv)

141   An external audit of XCD's financial statements has discovered that due to flooding of its administration offices a large proportion of XCD's financial records were destroyed. XCD's accountants have reconstructed the data to enable them to prepare the financial statements but there is insufficient evidence to enable the auditors to verify most of the sales and purchase transactions during the year.

Which TWO of the following types of audit report and opinion would be appropriate?

A   Unmodified report

B   Modified report

C   Disclaimer of opinion

D   Adverse opinion

E   Qualified opinion

142   C is a small developing country which passed legislation to create a recognised professional accounting body two years ago. At the same time as the accounting body was created, new regulations governing financial reporting requirements of entities were passed. However, there are currently no accounting standards in C.

C's government has asked the new professional accounting body to prepare a report setting out the country's options for developing and implementing a set of high quality local accounting standards. The government request also referred to the work of the IASB and its International Financial Reporting Standards.

Place the following options into the highlighted boxes in the table below to correctly explain ONE advantage and ONE disadvantage of each of the following options. The options cannot be used more than once.

Any standards developed will be specific to C's requirements
Quick to implement
It will not be quick to implement
Standards may not take into account any specific local traditions or variations
Standards should be more relevant to local needs and compliant with International Standards
It will take longer to implement and requires an adequate level of expertise to exist within the country

	Adopting International Financial Reporting Standards (IFRS) as its local standards	Modelling local accounting standards on the IASB's IFRSs, but amending them to reflect local needs and conditions	Develop its own accounting standards with little or no reference to IFRSs
Advantage			
Disadvantage			

143 **Place THREE of the following options into the highlighted boxes in the table below to correctly explain the purpose of The Conceptual Framework for Financial Reporting.**

Assist the IASB on agenda decisions and priorities in its work
Assist users of financial statements that are prepared using IFRSs
Assist the IASB in the development of future IFRSs and in its review of existing IFRSs
Assist auditors in forming an opinion as to whether financial statements conform with IFRSs
Assist directors when preparing budgets and allocating resources

The purpose of the Framework

144 AB's profits have suffered due to a slow-down in the economy of the country in which it operates. AB's draft financial statements show revenue of $35 million and profit before tax of $4 million for the year ended 31 December 20X9.

AB's external auditors have identified a significant quantity of inventory that is either obsolete or seriously impaired in value. The auditor senior has calculated the inventory write down of $1 million. AB's directors have been asked by the audit senior to record this in the financial statements for the year ended 31 December 20X9.

AB's directors are refusing to write-down the inventory at 31 December 20X9, claiming that they were not aware of any problems at that date and furthermore do not agree with the auditor that there may be a problem now. The directors are proposing to carry out a stock-take at 31 May 20Y0 and to calculate their own inventory adjustment, if required. If necessary the newly calculated figure will be used to adjust inventory values in the year to 31 December 20Y0.

Assuming that AB's directors continue to refuse to amend the financial statements, what type of audit report that would be appropriate for the auditor to issue?

A   Modified report with a qualified opinion

B   Modified report with an adverse opinion

C   Modified report with a disclaimer of opinion

D   Unmodified report with a qualified opinion

145 Generally accepted accounting practice (GAAP) in a country can be based on legislation and accounting standards that are either:

- Very prescriptive in nature; or

- Principle-based.

Place the following options into the highlighted boxes in the table below to correctly explain principle-based accounting standards and prescriptive standards.

The standard would require a certain treatment to be used, regardless of the situation
The standard would be applied using professional judgement
Flexible
Less flexible
Standards should ensure the spirit of the regulations are adhered to
Standards more likely to lead to the letter of the law being followed rather than the spirit

Principle-based accounting standards	Prescriptive accounting standards

146 The IASB's The Conceptual Framework for Financial Reporting provides definitions of the elements of financial statements. One of the elements defined by the Framework is income.

Complete the sentence below by placing one of the following options into the space.

Income is _____.

increases in economic benefits during the accounting period in the form of inflows or decreases of liabilities that result in increases in equity, other than those relating to combinations from equity participants
increases in economic benefits during the accounting period in the form of inflows or enhancements of assets; or decreases of liabilities that result in increases in equity, other than those relating to combinations from equity participants
increases in economic benefits during the accounting period in the form of inflows or enhancements of assets; or decreases of liabilities that result in increases in equity

147 Criteria must be met for assets and liabilities to be recognised in an entity's financial statements. To be recognised the item must meet the definition of an element and the two other criteria set by The Conceptual Framework for Financial Reporting.

Complete the sentence below by placing one of the following options into each of the spaces.

probable	likely
with accuracy	reasonably
possible	with reliability

In order to recognise items in the statement of financial position or statement of profit or loss, The Framework states the following criteria should be satisfied:

- it meets the definition of an element of financial statements

- it is _____ that any future economic benefit associated with the item will flow to or from the entity; and

- the item has a cost or value that can be measured _____.

Data for Questions 148 and 149

CX, a professional accountant is facing a dilemma. She is working on the preparation of a long term profit forecast required by the local stock market listing regulations prior to a new share issue of equity shares.

At a previous management board meeting, her projections had been criticised by board members as being too pessimistic. She was asked to review her assumptions and increase the profit projections.

She revised her assumptions, but this had only marginally increased the forecast profits.

At yesterday's board meeting the board members had discussed her assumptions and specified new values to be used to prepare a revised forecast. In her view the new values grossly overestimate the forecast profits.

The management board intends to publish the revised forecasts.

---

148 **Which TWO of following ethical principles does CX face?**

A   Integrity

B   Confidentiality

C   Professional care and due competence

D   Objectivity

E   Professional behaviour

149 **Place the following options into the highlighted boxes in the table below to correctly show the order CX should deal with an ethical dilemma.**

Report internally to immediate management
Report externally
Remove herself from the situation
Gather evidence and document the problem
Report internally to higher management

	Dealing with an ethical dilemma
1	
2	
3	
4	
5	

Data for Questions 150 and 151

You are the partner in charge of the audit of LMN. The following matter has been brought to your attention in the audit working papers.

During the year LMN spent $500,000 on applied research, trying to find an application for a new process it had developed. LMN's management has capitalised this expenditure. LMN management is refusing to change its accounting treatment as it does not want to reduce the year's profit. The draft financial statements show revenue of $40 million and net profit of $4.5 million.

150 **Place TWO of the following options into the highlighted boxes in the table below to correctly show the type of audit report that would be appropriate to the above statements, assuming that LMN's management continue to refuse to change the financial statements.**

Qualified
Modified
Adverse
Disclaimer of
Unmodified

Report	Opinion

151 **Which TWO of following statements are TRUE regarding materiality?**

A   A matter is material if its omission could influence the economic decisions of users

B   A matter is material if its misstatement could influence the economic decisions of users

C   A matter is material if its omission or misstatement could influence the economic decisions of users

D   Items can only be material due to their size

E   Items can be material due to their size or nature

Data for questions 152 and 153

RS, an employee, prepares monthly management accounting information for XYZ which includes detailed performance data that is used to calculate staff bonuses. Based on information prepared by RS this year's bonuses will be lower than expected.

RS has had approaches from other staff offering various incentives to make accruals for additional revenue and other reversible adjustments, to enable all staff (including RS) to receive increased or higher bonuses.

152 **Which TWO of following ethical principles does RS face?**

A   Integrity

B   Confidentiality

C   Professional care and due competence

D   Objectivity

E   Professional behaviour

153 **Which of following ethical threats does RS face?**

   A   Advocacy threat

   B   Self-review threat

   C   Intimidation threat

   D   Self-interest threat

154 There are the four main entities that are involved in developing and implementing International Accounting Standards.

   Place the following options into the highlighted boxes in the table below to correctly show one role of each of the four entities.

Provides timely guidance on the application and interpretation of IFRSs
Provides strategic advice to the IASB and informs the IASB of public views on major standard setting projects
Governance and fund raising
Responsibility for all technical matters including the preparation and publication of international financial reporting standards

IFRS Foundation	International Accounting Standards Board (IASB)	IFRS Advisory Council	IFRS Interpretations Committee

Data for Questions 155 and 156

XQ, an employee of ABC, prepares monthly management accounting information for ABC. This information includes detailed performance data that is used to evaluate managers' performance. The directors are considering the closure of some facilities and XQ's management information will be included in the review.

XQ has had approaches from a number of concerned managers offering various incentives to make adjustments to the management accounting information to improve their performance statistics.

155 **Which THREE of following ethical principles does XQ face?**

   A   Integrity

   B   Confidentiality

   C   Professional care and due competence

   D   Objectivity

   E   Professional behaviour

   F   Neutrality

156 XQ should document the situation and report it to whom in the first instance?

A CIMA

B Externally to shareholders

C Internally to an immediate manager

D Externally to a legal advisor

157 Which TWO of the following is NOT a benefit of an external audit?

A The financial statements will not have any errors in them

B Applications to third parties for finance may be enhanced

C Avoids breaking the law, for some entities an audit is not an option

D It is likely to act as a fraud deterrent

E The auditors will assist in the preparation of the financial statements

158 Ace is a management accountant working as part of a small team that has been set up by ZY, his employer, to evaluate tenders submitted for contracts being awarded by ZY.

He has just discovered that one of the other team members accepted large payments in exchange for information, from an entity at the time it was considering tendering. Ace suspects that this may have influenced the winning tender submitted by the entity.

Ace should document the situation and then report it internally to his line manager. If this is unsuccessful what should he do next?

A Report it to CIMA

B Report it externally to shareholders

C Report it internally to higher management

D Report it externally to a legal advisor

159 An external audit of VH's financial statements has discovered that a customer who, at 31 March 20X4, owed VH $250,000 was declared bankrupt on 8 April 20X4. VH has not provided for the irrecoverable debt in its financial statements for the year ended 31 March 20X4. This is regarded as material but not pervasive.

Assuming that the auditors find everything else satisfactory, which of the following is the appropriate audit report for the auditors of VH to issue?

A The external audit report should be a modified report, with a qualified 'except for opinion'

B The external audit report should be an unmodified report with an emphasis of matter paragraph relating to the bad debt

C The external audit report should be a modified report, with a disclaimer of opinion

D The external audit report should be a modified report, with an adverse opinion.

160 Under the current structure of regulatory bodies, which organisation is responsible for reviewing international reporting standards and issuing revised international reporting standards?

A   IFRS Advisory Council

B   IFRS Interpretations Committee

C   International Accounting Standards Board

D   IFRS Foundation

161 Which ONE of the following is NOT a fundamental principle of the CIMA Code of Ethics?

A   Objectivity

B   Integrity

C   Confidentiality

D   Responsibility

162 Which of the following are responsibilities of the IFRS Advisory Council?

(i)   Give advice to the IASB on agenda decisions and priorities in its work

(ii)   Annually review the strategy of the IASB

(iii) Inform the IASB of the views of the members of the Council on proposed new standards

(iv)   Appoint the members of the IASB

A   (i) and (ii)

B   (ii) and (iv)

C   (i) and (iii)

D   (iii) and (iv)

163 The IASB's Conceptual Framework for Financial Reporting identifies the fundamental and enhancing qualitative characteristics of financial statements.

Place the following options into the highlighted boxes in the table below to correctly show which are the fundamental and enhancing characteristics.

Relevance	Understandability
Comparability	Verifiability
Timeliness	Faithful representation

Fundamental	**Enhancing**

164 A customer of CDF went bankrupt on 15 January 20X4 owing CDF $75,000. CDF's profit for the year ended 31 December 20X3 was $750,000 and its statement of financial position at that date showed trade receivables of $300,000. CDF has not provided for any irrecoverable debts for the year ended 31 December 20X3. This is material but not pervasive.

Which of the following types of audit report should the external auditor of CDF issue for the financial statements of CDF for the year ended 31 December 20X3?

A   A modified report with a qualified opinion in respect of receivables

B   A modified report with a disclaimer opinion

C   A modified report with an adverse opinion

D   A modified report with an emphasis of matter paragraph

165 **Which of the following is NOT listed as an element of financial statements by the IASB Conceptual Framework for Financial Reporting?**

A   Asset

B   Equity

C   Profit

D   Expenses

166 The IASB's Conceptual Framework for Financial Reporting identifies faithful representation as a fundamental qualitative characteristic of financial information.

Which of the following is NOT a characteristic of faithful representation?

A   Free from error

B   Verifiable

C   Neutral

D   Complete

167 **Complete the sentence below by placing one of the following options into the space.**

The purpose of corporate governance is to protect the _____.

| directors |
| employees |
| shareholders |

168 **Complete the sentence below by placing one of the following options into each of the spaces.**

Corporate governance is the means by which a company is _____ and _____.

organised	taxed
operated	accounted for
created	controlled

169 The aim of corporate governance initiatives is to ensure that entities are run well in the interests of their shareholders and the wider community.

Which of the following does it NOT include?

A   The necessity for good internal control

B   The necessity for an audit committee

C   Relationships with the external auditors

D   Relationships with the internal auditors

170 There are different approaches to corporate governance, rules-based and principle-approach.

Place the following options into the highlighted boxes in the table below to correctly show the characteristics of each approach.

Comply with the code or explain why	Applied in the UK
Applied in the US	Penalties for transgression
Instils the code into law	Adhere to the spirit rather than the letter of the code

Rules-based	Principle-based

FINANCIAL ACCOUNTING AND REPORTING

171 In the statement of cash flow of BKS for the year to 31 December 20X5 the net cash flow from operating activities is to be arrived at by the indirect method.

The following information is relevant:

	$000
Profit before tax	12,044
Depreciation	1,796
Loss on sale of tangible non-current assets	12
Increase in inventories	398
Increase in receivables	144
Increase in payables	468

Calculate the cash generated from operations for the year ended 31 December 20X5.

$ _____. (Your answer should be rounded down to the nearest $.)

172 At 30 September 20X5, BY had the following balances, with comparatives:

Statement of financial position extracts

As at 30 September	20X5	20X4
	$000	$000
Non-current tangible assets		
Property, plant and equipment	260	180
Equity and reserves		
Property, plant and equipment revaluation reserve	30	10

The statement of profit or loss for the year ended 30 September 20X5 included:

Gain on disposal of an item of equipment	$10,000
Depreciation charge for the year	$40,000

Notes to the accounts:

Equipment disposed of had cost $90,000. The proceeds received on disposal were $15,000.

Calculate the property, plant and equipment purchases that BY would show in its statement of cash flow for the year ended 30 September 20X5, as required by IAS 7 Statement of Cash Flows.

$ _____. (Your answer should be rounded down to the nearest $.)

173 At 1 October 20X4, BK had the following balance:

Accrued interest payable $12,000 credit

During the year ended 30 September 20X5, BK charged interest payable of $41,000 to its statement of profit or loss. The closing balance on accrued interest payable account at 30 September 20X5 was $15,000 credit.

How much interest paid should BK show on its cash flow statement for the year ended 30 September 20X5?

A $38,000

B $41,000

C $44,000

D $53,000

174 There follows extracts from the financial statements of BET for the year to 31 March 20X5 (all figures are in $000).

Extract from the statement of profit or loss

	$000	$000
Profit on ordinary activities before taxation		1,600
Taxation		
Income taxes – current year	460	
– over provision in 20X4	(10)	
	———	(450)
		———
		1,150
		———

Extracts from the statement of financial position as at 31 March

	20X5	20X4
Current liabilities – taxation	560	460

Calculate the amount that will appear in respect of income taxes in the cash flow statement for the year to 31 March 20X5.

$ _____. (Your answer should be rounded down to the nearest $.)

175 The following balances were extracted from N's financial statements:

Extracts from the statement of financial position as at 31 December

	20X9	20X8
	$000	$000
Current liabilities		
Current tax payable	157	133

Extract from statement of profit or loss and other comprehensive income for the year ended 31 December 20X9

	$000
Income tax expense	122

The amount of tax paid that should be included in N's statement of cash flows for the year ended 31 December 20X9 is:

A $98,000

B $109,000

C $122,000

D $241,000

176 **Which TWO of the following would be shown in a statement of cash flow using the direct method but not in a statement of cash flow using the indirect method of calculating cash generated from operations?**

A   Cash payments to employees

B   Increase/(decrease) in receivables

C   Depreciation

D   Finance costs

E   Cash receipts from customers

177 IAS 7 Statement of Cash Flows sets out the three main headings to be used in a statement of cash flows.

Which THREE of the following items would be included under the heading Cash flows from operating activities according to IAS 7?

A   Tax paid

B   Purchase of investments

C   Loss on disposal of machinery

D   Purchase of equipment

E   Impairment of an asset

F   Proceeds from the sale of intangibles

178   According to IFRS 8 Operating Segments which TWO of the following apply to reportable segments?

(i)   The results of the segment must be prepared using the same accounting policies as are used for the financial statements.

(ii)   A reportable segment is a component of the entity whose operating results are regularly reviewed by the entity's chief operating decision maker in order to make decisions about resource allocations.

(iii)   Information for reportable segments is required to be prepared based on products and geographical areas.

(iv)   A reportable segment is every segment that accounts for 10% or more of the revenue.

A   (i) and (ii)

B   (i) and (iii)

C   (ii) and (iii)

D   (ii) and (iv)

179   Which of the following is NOT included in the definition of an operating segment in accordance with IFRS 8 Operating Segments?

A   A component of an entity that earns the majority of its revenue from sales to external customers

B   A component of an entity that engages in business activities from which it may earn revenues and incur expenses

C   A component of an entity whose operating results are regularly reviewed by the entity's chief operating decision maker, to make decisions about resource allocations and assess performance

D   A component of an entity for which discrete financial information is available

180 IFRS 8 Operating Segments requires information about operating segments to be disclosed in the financial statements.

According to IFRS 8 Operating Segments which of the following defines an operating segment?

An operating segment is a component of an entity

A   that is considered to be one of the entity's main products or services

B   whose operating results are regularly reviewed by the entity's chief operating decision maker

C   whose results contribute more than 10% of the entity's total sales revenue

D   whose assets are more than 10% of the entity's total assets

181 **Complete the sentence below by placing one of the following options into each of the three spaces.**

An operating segment is defined by IFRS 8 as a component of an entity whose _____ results are regularly reviewed by the entity's chief operating _____ to make decisions about resources to be allocated to the segment and assess its _____.

profitability	performance
financial	operating
decision maker	officer

182 **According to IAS 8, how should a material error in the previous financial reporting period be accounted for in the current period?**

A   By making an adjustment in the financial statements of the current period through the statement of profit or loss, and disclosing the nature of the error in a note

B   By making an adjustment in the financial statements of the current period as a movement on reserves, and disclosing the nature of the error in a note

C   By restating the comparative amounts for the previous period at their correct value, and disclosing the nature of the error in a note

D   By restating the comparative amounts for the previous period at their correct value, but without the requirement for a disclosure of the nature of the error in a note

183 **According to IAS 8 Accounting Policies, Changes in Accounting Estimates and Errors, which of the following would require a prior period adjustment in JE's financial statements for the year ended 31 October 20X9?**

A   Inventory at 31 October 20X8 had been materially over-valued due to an error in the year-end inventory count that caused inventory in one warehouse to be counted twice

B   The straight line method of depreciation used to depreciate vehicles up to 31 October 20X8 was changed by JE to reducing balance method from 1 November 20X8

C   JE acquired a business from a sole trader on 1 December 20X0. JE amortised the goodwill over 20 years. On 1 November 20X8 JE ceased amortisation of goodwill as required by IFRS 3 Business Combinations

D   On 1 November 20X8, JE decided to change the method of calculating attributable profit recognized on uncompleted construction contracts from the percentage of cost method to the percentage of work completed method

184 According to IAS 8, there are TWO circumstances when a change in accounting policy permitted.

Place TWO of the following options into the highlighted boxes in the table below to correctly show these two circumstances.

Required by a change in management of the organisation
Required by a new or revised accounting standard
Results in will be more comparable to other group members
Results in financial statements will provide more reliable and more relevant information

Change in policy

185 During its 20X6 accounting year, DL made the following changes.

Which of these changes would be classified as a change in accounting policy as determined by IAS 8 Accounting Policies, Changes in Accounting Estimates and Errors?

A   Increased the irrecoverable debt provision for 20X6 from 5% to 10% of outstanding debts

B   Changed the treatment of borrowing costs from expensing borrowing costs incurred on capital projects to capitalising all borrowing costs in the year incurred

C   Changed the depreciation of plant and equipment from straight line depreciation to reducing balance depreciation

D   Changed the useful economic life of its motor vehicles from six years to four years

186 **According to IAS 8 Accounting Policies, Changes in Accounting Estimates and Errors, which TWO of the following are errors requiring a retrospective adjustment in financial statements for the year ended 31 December 20X1?**

A   The useful life of an asset has been reviewed and changed from a 10 year remaining life to 8 years

B   The depreciation method of vehicles was changed from straight line depreciation to reducing balance

C   The provision for warranty claims was changed from 10% of sales revenue to 5%

D   Based on information that became available in the current period a provision was made for an injury compensation claim relating to an incident in a previous year

E   Inventory at 31 December 20X0 had been materially over-valued due to an error in the year-end inventory count that caused inventory in one warehouse to be counted twice

187 **Which of the following would be regarded as a change of accounting estimate according to IAS 8 Accounting Policies, Changes in Accounting Estimates and Errors?**

   A   An entity started capitalising borrowing costs for assets as required by IAS 23 Borrowing Costs. Borrowing costs had previously been charged to the statement of profit or loss

   B   An entity started revaluing its properties, as allowed by IAS 16 Property, Plant and Equipment. Previously all property, plant and equipment had been carried at cost less accumulated depreciation

   C   A material error in the inventory valuation methods caused the closing inventory at 31 March 20X8 to be overstated by $900,000

   D   An entity created a provision for claims under its warranty of products sold during the year. 5% of sales revenue had previously been set as the required provision amount. After an analysis of three years sales and warranty claims the calculation of the provision amount has been changed to a more realistic 2% of sales

188 CI purchased equipment on 1 April 20X2 for $100,000. The equipment was depreciated using the reducing balance method at 25% per year. CI's reporting date is 31 March.

Depreciation was charged up to and including 31 March 20X6. At that date, the recoverable amount was $28,000.

Calculate the impairment loss on the equipment according to IAS 36 Impairment of Assets for the year to 31 March 20X6.

$ _____. (Your answer should be rounded down to the nearest $.)

Data for Questions 189 and 190

DOC purchased property for $320,000 exactly 10 years ago. The land included in the price was valued at $120,000. The property was estimated to have a useful economic life of 20 years.

DOC has now had the property revalued (for the first time) by a professional valuer. The total value had increased to $800,000, the land now being valued at $200,000. The useful economic life remained unchanged.

---

189 **Calculate the amount that should be credited to DOC's revaluation reserve.**

$ _____. (Your answer should be rounded down to the nearest $.)

190 **Calculate annual depreciation charge on the property in future years.**

$ _____. (Your answer should be rounded down to the nearest $.)

191 **Which of the following gives the best definition of Property, Plant and Equipment, based on the provisions of IAS 16?**

A   Any assets held by an enterprise for more than one accounting period for use in the production or supply of goods or services, for rental to others, or for administrative purposes

B   Tangible assets held by an enterprise for more than 12 months for use in the production or supply of goods or services, for rental to others, or for administrative purposes

C   Tangible assets held by an enterprise for more than one accounting period for use in the production or supply of goods or services, for rental to others, or for administrative purposes

D   Any assets held by an enterprise for more than 12 months for use in the production or supply of goods or services, for rental to others, or for administrative purposes

192   JT is registered with its local tax authority and can reclaim value added tax paid on items purchased.

During the year JT purchased a large machine from another country. The supplier invoiced JT as follows:

	$
Cost of basic machine	100,000
Special modifications made to basic design	15,000
Supplier's engineer's time installing and initial testing of machine	2,000
Three years' maintenance and servicing	21,000
	138,000
Value added tax @ 20%	27,600
	165,600

Prior to delivery, JT spent $12,000 preparing a heavy duty concrete base for the machine.

Calculate the amount that JT should debit to non-current assets for the cost of the machine.

$ _____. (Your answer should be rounded down to the nearest $.)

193 **Which of the following statements is correct?**

Statement 1: If the revaluation model is used for property, plant and equipment, revaluations must subsequently be made with sufficient regularity to ensure that the carrying amount does not differ materially from the fair value at each reporting date.

Statement 2: When an item of property, plant and equipment is revalued, there is no requirement that the entire class of assets to which the item belongs must be revalued.

A   Statement 1 only is correct

B   Statement 2 only is correct

C   Both statements are correct

D   Neither statement is correct

194 F's year-end is 30 June. F purchased a non-current asset for $50,000 on 1 July 20X2.

Depreciation was provided at the rate of 20% per annum on the straight-line basis. There was no forecast residual value.

On 1 July 20X4, the asset was revalued to $60,000 and then depreciated on a straight-line basis over its remaining useful economic life which was unchanged. On 1 July 20X5, the asset was sold for $35,000.

In addition to the entries in the non-current asset account and provision for depreciation account, which TWO of the following statements correctly record the entries required on disposal of the non-current asset?

A   Debit statement of profit or loss with a loss on disposal of $5,000

B   Credit statement of profit or loss with a gain on disposal of $25,000

C   Transfer $60,000 from revaluation reserve to retained earnings as a movement on reserves

D   Transfer $30,000 from revaluation reserve to retained earnings as a movement on reserves

E   Transfer $30,000 from revaluation reserve to statement of profit or loss

195 **Which of the following items would CM recognise as subsequent expenditure on a non-current asset and capitalise it as required by IAS 16 Property, Plant and Equipment?**

A   CM purchased a furnace five years ago, when the furnace lining was separately identified in the accounting records. The furnace now requires relining at a cost of $200,000. When the furnace is relined it will be able to be used in CM's business for a further five years

B   CM's office building has been badly damaged by a fire. CM intends to restore the building to its original condition at a cost of $250,000

C   CM's delivery vehicle broke down. When it was inspected by the repairers it was discovered that it needed a new engine. The engine and associated labour costs are estimated to be $5,000

D   CM closes its factory for two weeks every year. During this time, all plant and equipment has its routine annual maintenance check and any necessary repairs are carried out. The cost of the current year's maintenance check and repairs was $75,000

196 DS purchased a machine on 1 October 20X2 at a cost of $21,000 with an expected useful economic life of six years, with no expected residual value. DS depreciates its machines using the straight line basis.

The machine has been used and depreciated for three years to 30 September 20X5. New technology was invented in December 20X5, which enabled a cheaper, more efficient machine to be produced; this technology makes DS's type of machine obsolete. The obsolete machine will generate no further economic benefit or have any residual value once the new machines become available. However, because of production delays, the new machines will not be available on the market until 1 October 20X7.

Calculate how much depreciation DS should charge to its statement of profit or loss for the year ended 30 September 20X6, as required by IAS 16 Property, Plant and Equipment.

$ _____. (Your answer should be rounded down to the nearest $.)

197 An item of plant and equipment was purchased on 1 April 20X1 for $100,000. At the date of acquisition its expected useful economic life was ten years. Depreciation was provided on a straight line basis, with no residual value.

On 1 April 20X3, the asset was revalued to $95,000. On 1 April 20X4, the useful life of the asset was reviewed and the remaining useful economic life was reduced to five years, a total useful life of eight years.

Calculate the carrying amount at 31 March 20X5, as required by IAS 16 Property, Plant and Equipment.

$ _____. (Your answer should be rounded down to the nearest $.)

198 IAS 16 Property, Plant and Equipment requires an asset to be measured at cost on its original recognition in the financial statements.

EW used its own staff, assisted by contractors when required, to construct a new warehouse for its own use.

Which of the following costs would NOT be included in attributable costs of the non-current asset?

A   Clearance of the site prior to work commencing

B   Professional surveyors' fees for managing the construction work

C   EW's own staff wages for time spent working on the construction

D   An allocation of EW's administration costs, based on EW staff time spent on the construction as a percentage of the total staff time

199 GK purchased a piece of development land on 31 October 20X0 for $500,000. GK revalued the land on 31 October 20X4 to $700,000. The latest valuation report, dated 31 October 20X8, values the land at $450,000.

GK has adjusted the land balance shown in non-current assets at 31 October 20X8.

Which of the following shows the correct debit entry in GK's financial statements for the year ended 31 October 20X8?

A   Dr   Revaluation reserve $50,000   and   Dr   Statement of profit $200,000
                                                   or loss

B   Dr   Revaluation reserve $250,000

C   Dr   Revaluation reserve $200,000   and   Dr   Statement of profit $50,000
                                                   or loss

D   Dr   Statement of profit or $250,000
                 loss

200 On 1 July 20X4, Experimenter opened a chemical reprocessing plant. The plant was due to be active for five years until 30 June 20X9, when it would be decommissioned. At 1 July 20X4, the costs of decommissioning the plant were estimated to be $4 million. The company considers that a discount rate of 12% is appropriate for the calculation of a present value, and the discount factor at 12% for Year 5 is 0.567.

What is the total charge to the statement of profit or loss (depreciation and finance charge) in respect of the decommissioning for the year ended 30 June 20X5?

A $453,600

B $725,760

C $800,000

D $2,268,000

201 An entity purchased an item of property for $6 million on 1 July 20X3. The value of the land was $1 million and the buildings $5 million. The expected life of the building was 50 years and its residual value nil. On 30 June 20X5 the property was revalued to $7 million (land $1.24 million, buildings $5.76 million). On 30 June 20X7, the property was sold for $6.8 million.

Which TWO of the following are true regarding the treatment of the disposal of the property for the year to 30 June 20X7?

A Gain on disposal of $40,000

B Gain on disposal of $200,000

C Gain on disposal of $84,800

D Release the revaluation reserve of $1,240,000

E Release the revaluation reserve of $1,200,000

202 **Which of the following CANNOT be recognised as an intangible non-current asset in GHK's statement of financial position at 30 September 20X1?**

A GHK spent $12,000 researching a new type of product. The research is expected to lead to a new product line in 3 years' time

B GHK purchased another entity, BN on 1 October 20X0. Goodwill arising on the acquisition was $15,000

C GHK purchased a brand name from a competitor on 1 November 20X0, for $65,000

D GHK spent $21,000 during the year on the development of a new product. The product is being launched on the market on 1 December 20X1 and is expected to be profitable

203 On 1 January Year 1, an entity purchased an item of equipment costing $76,000. The asset is depreciated using the reducing balance method, at a rate of 20% each year. After three years, an impairment review establishes that the asset has a value in use of $30,000 and a disposal value (less selling costs) of $27,000.

Calculate the amount of the impairment loss that should be written off in the statement of profit or loss for the year to 31 December Year 3.

$ _____.(Your answer should be rounded down to the nearest $.)

204 The information below refers to three non-current assets of IDLE as at 31 March 20X5:

	A	B	C
	$000	$000	$000
Carrying amount	200	300	240
Net selling price	220	250	200
Value in use	240	260	180

What is the total impairment loss?

A $40,000

B $80,000

C $90,000

D $110,000

Data for Questions 205 and 206

X acquired the business and assets from the owners of an unincorporated business: the purchase price was satisfied by the issue of 10,000 equity shares with a nominal value of $10 each and $20,000 cash. The market value of X shares at the date of acquisition was $20 each.

The assets acquired were:

- net tangible non-current assets with a book value of $20,000 and a current value of $25,000

- patents for a specialised process valued by a specialist valuer at $15,000

- brand name, valued by a specialist brand valuer on the basis of a multiple of earnings at $50,000

- publishing rights of the first text from an author that the management of X expects to become a best seller. The publishing rights were a gift from the author to the previous owners at no cost. The management of X has estimated the future value of the potential best seller at $100,000. However, there is no reliable evidence available to support the estimate of the management.

---

205 **What is the correct accounting treatment to be used for the publishing rights of the first text?**

Place TWO of the following options into the highlighted boxes in the table below to correctly show the correct treatment.

The rights do not meet the definition of an asset as we do not have a reliable cost
The rights do meet the definition of an asset as we have a reliable cost
Capitalise the rights as an intangible asset at $100,000
Expense the rights to the statement of profit or loss at $100,000

Treatment of publishing rights

206 **Calculate the value of goodwill to be included in the accounts of X for this purchase.**

$ _____. (Your answer should be rounded down to the nearest $.)

207 IAS 38 Intangible Assets sets out six criteria that must be met before an internally generated intangible asset can be recognised.

Place THREE of the following options into the highlighted boxes in the table below to correctly show THREE of IAS 38's criteria for recognition.

Revenues can be measured
Adequate cash to complete
An intention to complete the project
Costs can be measured
An ability to use or sell the developed item
The developed item with generate a probable future economic benefit

IAS 38's criteria for recognition

208 **Which of the following statements does NOT comply with standard accounting practice in respect of the accounting treatment of purchased goodwill?**

A   If there is an impairment in value of purchased goodwill, the amount of the impairment should be taken directly to the reserves and not through the statement of profit or loss

B   Purchased goodwill should not be revalued upwards

C   Purchased goodwill, insofar as it has not been written off, should be shown as a separate item under non-current assets in the statement of financial position

D   Purchased goodwill should not be amortised

209 A company has been carrying out work on the design and testing of a new product. The work began in May 20X1 and it is now the end of 20X3. From 31 December 20X1, the project to develop the new product met all the criteria in IAS 38 for the development costs to be recognised as an intangible asset.

The recoverable amount of the know-how embodied in the development work has been estimated as follows:

At 31 December 20X1: $400,000
At 31 December 20X2: $1,500,000
At 31 December 20X3: $2,000,000

The costs incurred on the project have been as follows:

Year to 31 December 20X1: $500,000
Year to 31 December 20X2: $1,000,000
Year to 31 December 20X3: $1,200,000

Calculate the expense that should be charged to the statement of profit or loss for the costs of the development project for the year to 31 December 20X3.

$ _____. (Your answer should be rounded down to the nearest $.)

210 **Which of the following could be classified as deferred development expenditure in M's statement of financial position as at 31 March 20X0 according to IAS 38 Intangible Assets?**

A $120,000 spent on developing a prototype and testing a new type of propulsion system for trains. The project needs further work on it as the propulsion system is currently not viable

B   A payment of $50,000 to a local university's engineering faculty to research new environmentally friendly building techniques

C $35,000 spent on consumer testing a new type of electric bicycle. The project is near completion and the product will probably be launched in the next twelve months. As this project is first of its kind for M it is expected to make a loss

D $65,000 spent on developing a special type of new packaging for a new energy efficient light bulb. The packaging is expected to be used by M for many years and is expected to reduce M's distribution costs by $35,000 a year

211 The following measures relate to a non-current asset:

(i)   carrying amount $20,000

(ii)   net realisable value $18,000

(iii)   value in use $22,000

(iv)   replacement cost $50,000.

The recoverable amount of the asset is:

A $18,000

B $20,000

C $22,000

D $50,000

212 Diva has tangible non-current assets in its statement of financial position at 31 December 20X4 and 31 December 20X5 as follows:

The following information is also available:

1   During the year, machines were disposed of for net sales proceeds of $20,000. The machines originally cost $125,000 and accumulated depreciation on the assets at the date of disposal was $111,000.

2   Assets under construction refer to a contract, started in November 20X4, to build and supply C with new machinery. The machinery was installed and testing was completed by 31 September 20X5. Production began early October 20X5. The balance on the assets under construction account was transferred to the plant and machinery account on 31 December 20X5. The amount transferred was $350,000.

Place the following options into the highlighted boxes in the table below to complete the disclosure note for property, plant and equipment for the year ended 31 December 20X5. The options can be used more than once and not all options have to be used.

(20)	0	772	(350)
(125)	(111)	1,459	125
145	403	1,550	111
350	9,876	863	20
1,240	890	297	2,115

Property, plant and equipment note 31 December 20X5

	Land	Buildings	Plant and machinery	Under construction	Total
Cost/valuation	$000	$000	$000	$000	$000
Balance at 1 January 20X5	2,743	3,177	1,538	53	7,511
Revaluation of assets	375	–	–	0	375
Disposal of assets	–	–		–	
Transfers	–	–			0
Additions	402	526			
Balance at 31 December 20X5	3,520	3,703	2,653		
Depreciation					
Balance at 1 January 20X5	–	612	671	–	1,283
Disposal of assets	–	–			
Depreciation for the year	–	75	212	–	287
Balance at 31 December 20X5	0	687		0	
Carrying amount 31 December 20X5	3,520	3,016	1,881	0	8,417
Carrying amount 31 December 20X4	2,743	2,565	867	53	6,228

213 Neville has only two items of inventory on hand at its reporting date.

Item 1 – Materials costing $24,000 bought for processing and assembly for a customer under a 'one off' order which is expected to produce a high profit margin. Since buying this material, the cost price has fallen to $20,000.

Item 2 – A machine constructed for another customer for a contracted price of $36,000. This has recently been completed at a cost of $33,600. It has now been discovered that, in order to meet certain health and safety regulations, modifications at an extra cost of $8,400 will be required. The customer has agreed to meet half the extra cost.

Calculate the total value of these two items of inventory in the statement of financial position.

$ _____.(Your answer should be rounded down to the nearest $.)

214 IAS 2 Inventories specifies expenses that should be included in year-end inventory values.

Which THREE of the following are allowable by IAS 2 as expenses that should be included in the cost of finished goods inventories?

A   Marketing and selling overhead

B   Variable production overhead

C   General management overhead

D   Accounting and finance overhead allocated to production

E   Cost of delivering raw materials to the factory

F   Abnormal increase in overhead charges caused by unusually low production levels due to the exceptionally hot weather

215 **Which of the following would be treated as a non-adjusting event after the reporting date, as required by IAS 10 Events after the Reporting Period, in the financial statements of AN for the period ended 31 January 20X5? The financial statements were approved for publication on 15 May 20X5.**

A   Notice was received on 31 March 20X5 that a major customer of AN had ceased trading and was unlikely to make any further payments

B   Inventory items at 31 January 20X5, original cost $30,000, were sold in April 20X5 for $20,000

C   During 20X4, a customer commenced legal action against AN. At 31 January 20X5, legal advisers were of the opinion that AN would lose the case, so AN created a provision of $200,000 for the damages claimed by the customer. On 27 April 20X5, the court awarded damages of $250,000 to the customer

D   There was a fire on 2 May 20X5 in AN's main warehouse which destroyed 50% of AN's total inventory

216 **Using the requirements set out in IAS 10 Events after the Reporting Period, which of the following would be classified as an adjusting event after the reporting period in financial statements ended 31 March 20X4 that were approved by the directors on 31 August 20X4?**

A   A reorganisation of the enterprise, proposed by a director on 31 January 20X4 and agreed by the Board on 10 July 20X4

B   A strike by the workforce which started on 1 May 20X4 and stopped all production for 10 weeks before being settled

C   A claim on an insurance policy for damage caused by a fire in a warehouse on 1 January 20X4. No provision had been made for the receipt of insurance money at 31 March 20X4 as it was uncertain that any money would be paid. The insurance enterprise settled with a payment of $1.5 million on 1 June 20X4

D   The enterprise had made large export sales to the USA during the year. The year end receivables included $2 million for amounts outstanding that were due to be paid in US dollars between 1 April 20X4 and 1 July 20X4. By the time these amounts were received, the exchange rate had moved in favour of the enterprise and the equivalent of $2.5 million was actually received

217 GD's financial reporting period is 1 September 20X7 to 31 August 20X8.

Which TWO of the following would be classified as a non-adjusting event according to IAS 10 Events after the Reporting Period?

Assume all amounts are material and that GD's financial statements have not yet been approved for publication.

A On 30 October 20X8, GD received a communication stating that one of its customers had ceased trading and gone into liquidation. The balance outstanding at 31 August 20X8 was unlikely to be paid

B At 31 August 20X8, GD had not provided for an outstanding legal action against the local government administration for losses suffered as a result of incorrect enforcement of local business regulations. On 5 November 20X8, the court awarded GD $50,000 damages

C On 1 October 20X8, GD made a share issue at a price of $1.75

D At 31 August 20X8, GD had an outstanding insurance claim of $150,000. On 10 October 20X8, the insurance company informed GD that it would pay $140,000 as settlement

E On 10 October 20X8 GD announced a plan to acquire DE in the next 12 months.

218 **Which of the following material items would be classified as a non-adjusting event in HL's financial statements for the year ended 31 December 20X8 according to IAS 10 Events after the Reporting Period?**

HL's financial statements were approved for publication on 8 April 20X9.

A On 1 March 20X9, HL's auditors discovered that, due to an error during the count, the closing inventory had been undervalued by $250,000

B Lightning struck one of HL's production facilities on 31 January 20X9 and caused a serious fire. The fire destroyed half of the factory and its machinery. Output was severely reduced for six months

C One of HL's customers commenced court action against HL on 1 December 20X8. At 31 December 20X8, HL did not know whether the case would go against it or not. On 1 March 20X9, the court found against HL and awarded damages of $150,000 to the customer

D On 15 March 20X9, HL was advised by the liquidator of one of its customers that it was very unlikely to receive any payments for the balance of $300,000 that was outstanding at 31 December 20X8

219 DT's final dividend for the year ended 31 October 20X5 of $150,000 was declared on 1 February 20X6 and paid in cash on 1 April 20X6. The financial statements were approved on 31 March 20X6.

Which TWO of the following statements reflect the correct treatment of the dividend?

A   The payment clears an accrued liability set up in the statement of financial position as at 31 October 20X5

B   The dividend is shown as a deduction in the statement of profit or loss for the year ended 31 October 20X6

C   The dividend is shown as an accrued liability in the statement of financial position as at 31 October 20X6

D   The $150,000 dividend was shown in the notes to the financial statements at 31 October 20X5

E   The dividend is shown as a deduction in the statement of changes in equity for the year ended 31 October 20X6

220 IAS 10 Events after the Reporting Period distinguishes between adjusting and non-adjusting events.

Place the following options into the highlighted boxes in the table below to correctly show which of the following items are adjusting events and which are non-adjusting events.

A dispute with workers caused all production to cease six weeks after the reporting date
A month after the reporting date XS's directors decided to cease production of one of its three product lines and to close the production facility
One month after the reporting date a court determined a case against XS and awarded damages of $50,000 to one of XS's customers. XS had expected to lose the case and had set up a provision of $30,000 at the reporting date
Three weeks after the reporting date a fire destroyed XS's main warehouse facility and most of its inventory
One month after the year end XS's main customer goes into liquidation owing XS a substantial amount of money
XS discovers a material error in the closing inventory value one month after the reporting date

Adjusting events	Non-adjusting events

221 N prepares financial statements to 31 December each year. On 30 November 20X4, N entered into a binding commitment to close a division on 31 January 20X5. The closure was completed on schedule and the following transactions occurred during January 20X5:

(i) N incurred closure costs of $4.2 million. $3 million of this figure was direct costs and $1.2 million was apportioned head office costs.

(ii) The division made a small operating profit of $300,000.

(iii) The division sold plant and made a loss on sale of $1,000,000. This fall in value had occurred before 31 December 20X4.

(iv) The division sold properties and made a profit on sale of $2,000,000.

The 20X4 financial statements were approved by the directors on 20 February 20X5.

Calculate the amount reported in the statement of profit or loss of N for the year ended 31 December 20X4 in respect of the closure of the division, in compliance with IFRS 5 Non-current Assets Held for Sale and Discontinued Operations.

$ _____. (Your answer should be rounded down to the nearest $)

222 BN has an asset that was classified as held for sale at 31 March 20X2. The asset had a carrying amount of $900 and a fair value of $800. The cost of disposal was estimated to be $50.

According to IFRS 5 Non-current Assets Held for Sale and Discontinued Operations, which of the following values should be used for the asset in BN's statement of financial position as at 31 March 20X2?

A $750

B $800

C $850

D $900

223 IAS 1 Presentation of Financial Statements encourages an analysis of expenses to be presented on the face of the statement of profit or loss. The analysis of expenses must use a classification based on either the nature of expense, or its function, within the entity.

Which TWO of the following would be disclosed on the face of the statement of profit or loss if a manufacturing entity uses analysis based on function?

A   Raw materials and consumables used

B   Distribution costs

C   Employee benefit costs

D   Cost of sales

E   Depreciation and amortisation expense.

Data for Questions 224 to 226

The following is an extract from the trial balance of CE at 31 March 20X6:

	$000	$000
Administrative expenses	260	
Cost of sales	480	
Interest paid	110	
10% Interest bearing borrowings		2,200
Inventory at 31 March 20X6	220	
Property, plant and equipment at cost	1,500	
Property, plant and equipment, depreciation to 31 March 20X5		540

Notes:

(i)   Included in the closing inventory at the reporting date was inventory at a cost of $35,000, which was sold during April 20X6 for $19,000.

(ii)   Depreciation is provided for on property, plant and equipment at 20% per year using the reducing balance method. Depreciation is regarded as cost of sales.

(iii)   A member of the public was seriously injured while using one of CE's products on 4 October 20X5. Professional legal advice is that CE will probably have to pay $500,000 compensation.

(iv)   The interest bearing borrowings were issued many years ago.

---

224   **Calculate the cost of sales expense for year ended 31 March 20X6.**

$ _____ . (Your answer should be rounded down to the nearest $)

225   **Calculate the administrative expense for year ended 31 March 20X6.**

$ _____ . (Your answer should be rounded down to the nearest $)

226   **Calculate the finance cost for year ended 31 March 20X6.**

$ _____ . (Your answer should be rounded down to the nearest $)

227   **Which of the following must be presented on the face of the statement of profit or loss?**

(i)   Finance charges

(ii)   Profits, gains and losses relating to discontinued operations

A   (i) only

B   (ii) only

C   Both (i) and (ii)

D   Neither

228 **Which of the following is NOT required by IAS 1 as an item to include in the notes to the accounts?**

A   A statement that the entity is a going concern

B   A statement of compliance with International Financial Reporting Standards

C   The dividends declared or proposed before the publication of the financial statements but not included in the statements as a distribution to shareholders in the period

D   The key sources of estimation uncertainty in the financial statements

229 IAS 1 Presentation of Financial Statements requires some of the items to be disclosed on the face of the financial statements and others to be disclosed in the notes.

Which TWO of the following have to be shown on the face of the statement of profit or loss, rather than in the notes?

A   Depreciation

B   Revenue

C   Closing inventory

D   Finance cost

E   Dividends

230 An entity undertakes a revaluation of its freehold property during the current period. The revaluation results in a significant surplus over carrying amount.

In which of the components of the current period financial statements required by IAS 1 would the revaluation surplus appear?

A   Statement of financial position and statement of changes in equity

B   Statement of changes in equity and statement of cash flow

C   Statement of financial position and statement of profit or loss

D   Statement of financial position and statement of cash flow

Data for Questions 231 to 233

The following financial information relates to FC for the year ended 31 March 20X8.

Statement of profit or loss for the year ended 31 March 20X8

	$000
Revenue	445
Cost of sales	(220)
	____
Gross profit	225
Other income	105
	____
	330
Administrative expense	(177)
	____
	153
Finance costs	(20)
	____
Profit before tax	133
Income tax expense	(43)
	____
Profit	90

The following administrative expenses were incurred in the year:

	$000
Wages	70
Other general expenses	15
Depreciation	92
	____
	177
	____

Other income:

	$000
Rentals received	45
Gain on disposal of non-current assets	60
	____
	105
	____

Statements of financial position extracts at:

	31 March 20X8	31 March 20X7
	$000	$000
Inventories	40	25
Trade receivables	50	45
Trade payables	(30)	(20)

231 Calculate the cash received from customers to be shown in the statement of cash flow for the year ended 31 March 20X8, in accordance with the direct method IAS 7 Statement of Cash Flows.

$ _____. (Your answer should be rounded down to the nearest $.)

232 Calculate the cash paid to suppliers to be shown the statement of cash flow for the year ended 31 March 20X8, in accordance with the direct method IAS 7 Statement of Cash Flows.

$ _____. (Your answer should be rounded down to the nearest $.)

233 Place the following options into the highlighted boxes in the table below to correctly calculate the cash generated from operations in accordance with the indirect method IAS 7 Statement of Cash Flows. The options cannot be used more than once and not all options have to be used.

20	(20)	15	(15)
92	(92)	5	(5)
60	(60)	10	(10)
175	295	195	215

FC's statement of cash flow YE 31 March 20X8	$000
Profit before tax	133
Finance cost	
Depreciation	
Gain on disposal of assets	
Inventory	
Receivables	
Payables	
	___
Cash generated from operations	
	___

Data for Questions 234 and 235

WZ is an assistant accountant with ABC. On 31 March 20X1 ABC decided to sell a property. This property was correctly classified as held for sale in accordance with IFRS 5 Non-current Assets Held For Sale and Discontinued Operations.

In its draft financial statements ABC has written down the property by $3.4 million. The write down was charged to the statement of profit or loss for the year ended 31 August 20X1. The draft financial statements showed a loss of $1.3 million for the year to 31 August 20X1.

When the management board of ABC reviewed the draft financial statements the board members were unhappy that the draft statements showed a loss and decided that the property should continue to be shown under non-current assets at its previous carrying amount.

234 **Which TWO of the following statements correctly show how WZ ethically treat the asset?**

    A   The asset should be shown under PPE until the asset is sold

    B   The asset should continue to be depreciated until it is sold

    C   The asset should be shown separately under assets held for sale

    D   Depreciation should cease at 31 March 20X1

    E   Depreciation should cease at 31 August 20X1

235 **Which TWO of the following ethical principles is WZ facing if he follows the management boards advice?**

    A   Integrity

    B   Confidentiality

    C   Professional behaviour

    D   Objectivity

    E   Reliability

236 A new type of delivery vehicle, when purchased on 1 April 20X0 for $20,000, was expected to have a useful economic life of four years. At 1 April 20X2 it was discovered that the original estimate of the useful economic life was too short, and the vehicle is now expected to have a useful economic life of six years from the date of purchase. All delivery vehicles are depreciated using the straight-line method and are assumed to have zero residual value.

Place TWO of the following options into the highlighted boxes in the table below to correctly show the correct treatment of an asset with a change in useful life.

A change in useful life is treated as a change in estimate as per IAS 8 Accounting Policies, Changes in Accounting Estimates and Errors
A change in useful life is treated as a change in policy as per IAS 8 Accounting Policies, Changes in Accounting Estimates and Errors
A change in useful life is treated as an error as per IAS 8 Accounting Policies, Changes in Accounting Estimates and Errors
Depreciation charge for 31 March 20X3 should be $1,667
Depreciation charge for 31 March 20X3 should be $2,500
Depreciation charge for 31 March 20X3 should be $3,333

	Change in useful life of an asset
Characteristic	
Characteristic	

237   CD is a manufacturing entity that runs a number of operations including a bottling plant that bottles carbonated soft drinks. CD has been developing a new bottling process that will allow the bottles to be filled and sealed more efficiently. The new process took a year to develop. At the start of development, CD estimated that the new process would increase output by 15% with no additional cost (other than the extra bottles and their contents). Development work commenced on 1 May 20X5 and was completed on 20 April 20X6. Testing at the end of the development confirmed CD's original estimates.

CD incurred expenditure of $180,000 on the above development in 20X5/X6.

CD plans to install the new process in its bottling plant and start operating the new process from 1 May 20X6.

CD's statement of financial position date is 30 April.

Complete the sentence below by placing one of the following options into each of the spaces.

CD should _____ the development costs and they should be shown as an _____ on the _____ for the year ended 30 April 20X6.

write off	expense
capitalise	intangible asset
statement of financial position	statement of profit or loss

238   Selected balances in HF's financial records at 30 April 20X8 were as follows:

	$000
Revenue	15,000
Profit	1,500
Property, plant and equipment – carrying value	23,000
Inventory	1,500

After completing the required audit work the external auditors of HF had the following observations:

(a)   Inventory with a book value of $500 is obsolete and should be written off.

(b)   Development expenditure carrying amount of $600,000, relating to the development of a new product line, had been capitalised and amortised in previous years but the project has now been abandoned.

Assume there are no other material matters outstanding.

An external auditor you have just completed a meeting with HF management. At the meeting HF management decided the following:

•   Item (1) is not material, so it is not necessary to write off the obsolete inventory.

•   Item (2) the development expenditure should be written off against current year profits.

Which of TWO of the following statements are true regarding the management's decisions taken in the meeting for items (1) and (2)?

A   Inventory has been overvalued by $500 and should be written off against current year profits

B   Inventory has been overvalued by $500 but it is not material and can be written off in the following year

C   It is not necessary to write off the obsolete inventory because it is not material

D   The development expenditure should be written off against current year profits

E   The development expenditure should be written off against previous year profits

F   The development expenditure can be continued to be capitalised until fully amortised

---

Data for Questions 239 to 241

JX acquired the business and assets of a sole trader for $700,000 on 1 November 20X8.

The fair values of the identifiable assets acquired were:

	$000
Non-current intangible assets	
Brand Z – brand name	200
Deferred development expenditure	90
Non-current tangible assets	
Plant and equipment	350
Current assets	
Inventory	10
	650

The deferred development expenditure related to expenditure incurred on development of a new product. After the acquisition JX continued developing this new product and spent a further $500,000 completing the development and getting the product ready for market. The product was launched on 1 November 20X9. The new product is expected to generate significant profits for JX over the next five years.

On 31 October 20X9 brand Z was independently valued at $250,000.

---

239   **Which THREE of the following statements explain how should JX treat the goodwill in its financial statements for the year ended 31 October 20X9?**

A   Goodwill should treated as an expense to the statement of profit or loss in the year of acquisition

B   Goodwill should be recognised as an intangible asset in the statement of financial position

C   Goodwill should be amortised over its useful life

D   Goodwill should be subject to an impairment review each year

E   Goodwill should be valued at $50,000

F   Goodwill should be valued at $700,000

240 Which THREE of the following statements explain how should JX treat the development expenditure in its financial statements for the year ended 31 October 20X9?

  A   Capitalise $590,000 as an intangible asset in the statement of financial position

  B   Development costs can only be capitalised if all of the criteria of IAS 38 is met

  C $500,000 development costs cannot be capitalised until 1 November 20X9

  D   Development costs will be amortised from 1 November 20X9

  E   Development costs will be amortised for the year ended 31 October 20X9

  F   Development costs can be capitalised if any of the criteria of IAS 38 is met

241 Which TWO of the following statements explain how should JX treat Brand Z in its financial statements for the year ended 31 October 20X9?

  A   Capitalise as an intangible asset in the statement of financial position

  B   Brands cannot be recognised

  C   Value at $200,000

  D   Value at $250,000

  E   Internally generated brands can be recognised

242 MN obtained a licence free of charge from the government to dig and operate a gold mine.

On the 31 October 20X9 there was a massive earthquake in the area and MN's mine shaft was badly damaged. It is estimated that the mine will be closed for at least six months and will cost $1 million to repair.

How should MN treat the effects of the earthquake in its financial statements for the year ended 31 August 20X9 in accordance with IAS 10 Events after the Reporting Period?

  A   Treat as an adjusting event with a disclosure note

  B   Treat as a non-adjusting event with a disclosure note

  C   Treat as a non-adjusting event without a disclosure note

  D   Treat as an adjusting event without a disclosure note

243 On 1 September 20X7, the Directors of EK decided to sell EK's retailing division and concentrate activities entirely on its manufacturing division.

The retailing division was available for immediate sale, but EK had not succeeded in disposing of the operation by 31 October 20X7. EK identified a potential buyer for the retailing division, but negotiations were at an early stage. The Directors of EK are certain that the sale will be completed by 31 August 20X8.

The retailing division's carrying value at 31 August 20X7 was:

	$000
Non-current tangible assets – property, plant and equipment	300
Non-current tangible assets – goodwill	100
Net current assets	43
Total carrying amount	443

The retailing division has been valued at $423,000, comprising:

	$000
Non-current tangible assets – property, plant and equipment	320
Non-current tangible assets – goodwill	60
Net current assets	43
Total carrying amount	423

EK's directors have estimated that EK will incur consultancy and legal fees for the disposal of $25,000.

Place FOUR of the following options into the highlighted boxes in the table below to correctly show the correct treatment of the discontinued operation according to IFRS 5 Non-current Assets Held for Sale and Discontinued Operations, for the year ended 31 October 20X7.

The assets have not met the criteria of an asset held for sale
The assets have met the criteria of an asset held for sale
EK should continue to show the assets in their normal categories in the statement of financial position
The assets should be shown separately as assets held for sale in the statement of financial position
The assets should be valued at $443,000
The assets should be valued at $423,000
The assets should be valued at $398,000
Impairment of $45,000 should be treated as an expense to the statement of profit or loss
Impairment of $20,000 should be treated as an expense to the statement of profit or loss
There is no impairment at the year ended 31 October 20X7

Treatment of the discontinued operation

Data for Questions 244 to 246

Extracts from CFQ's Statement of financial position at 31 March 20X3, with comparatives appear below:

	31 March 20X3	31 March 20X2
	$ million	$ million
Property, plant and equipment	635	645
Non-current asset investments at fair value	93	107
Deferred development expenditure	29	24

During the year to 31 March 20X3, CFQ sold property, plant and equipment for $45m. It had originally cost $322m and had a carrying amount of $60m at the date of disposal.

CFQ's statement of profit or loss for the year ended 31 March 20X3 included:

- depreciation of property, plant and equipment of $120m

- amortisation of deferred development expenditure of $8m

- revaluation loss on investments of $21m.

244 **Calculate the purchases of property, plant and equipment to be shown in the investing activities section of the statement of cash flow for the year ended 31 March 20X3, in accordance with IAS 7 Statement of Cash Flows.**

$ _____. (Your answer should be rounded down to the nearest $ million)

245 **Calculate the purchases of non-current asset investments to be shown in the investing activities section of the statement of cash flow for the year ended 31 March 20X3, in accordance with IAS 7 Statement of Cash Flows.**

$ _____. (Your answer should be rounded down to the nearest $ million)

246 **Calculate the purchases of deferred development expenditure to be shown in the investing activities section of the statement of cash flow for the year ended 31 March 20X3, in accordance with IAS 7 Statement of Cash Flows.**

$ _____. (Your answer should be rounded down to the nearest $ million)

247 EK publishes various types of book and occasionally produces films which it sells to major film distributors.

(i) On 31 March 20X7, EK acquired book publishing and film rights to the next book to be written by an internationally acclaimed author, for $1 million. The author has not yet started writing the book, but expects to complete it in 20X9.

(ii) Between 1 June and 31 July 20X7, EK spent $500,000 exhibiting its range of products at a major international trade fair. This was the first time EK had attended this type of event. No new orders were taken as a direct result of the event, although EK directors claim to have made valuable contacts that should generate additional sales or additional funding for films in the future. No estimate can be made of additional revenue at present.

(iii) During the year, EK employed an external consultant to redesign EK's corporate logo and to create advertising material to improve EK's corporate image. The total cost of the consultancy was $800,000.

EK's directors want to treat all of the above items of expenditure as assets for year ended 31 October 20X7.

Place the following options into the highlighted boxes in the table below to correctly show the correct treatment of the three items of expenditure for year ended 31 October 20X7. The options can be used more than once and not all options have to be used.

| Treat as an intangible asset |
| Expense to the statement of profit or loss |
| Do not amortise in current year |
| Criteria of IAS 38 not met to capitalise |
| Amortise |

Item (i)	Item (ii)	Item (iii)

248 You are in charge of the preparation of the financial statements for DF. You are nearing completion of the preparation of the accounts for the year ended 30 September 20X6 and the following item has come to your attention.

Shortly after a senior employee left DF in April 20X6, a number of accounting discrepancies were discovered. With further investigation, it became clear that fraudulent activity had been going on. DF has calculated that, because of the fraud, the profit for the year ended 30 September 20X5 had been overstated by $45,000.

Which THREE of the following statements explains how DF should treat this item?

A   DF should show the adjustment in the statement of profit or loss for year ended 30 September 20X6

B   DF should reduce the retained earnings for year ended 30 September 20X5 in the statement of changes in equity in the for year ended 30 September 20X6

C   A disclosure note should be provided for year ended 30 September 20X6

D   DF should not show the adjustment in the statement of profit or loss for year ended 30 September 20X6

E   A disclosure note should be provided for year ended 30 September 20X5

F   DF should reduce the retained earnings for year ended 30 September 20X5 in the statement of changes in equity for the year ended 30 September 20X5

Data for Questions 249 to 252

DV purchased two buildings on 1 September 20W6. Building A cost $200,000 and had a useful economic life of 20 years. Building B cost $120,000 and had a useful economic life of 15 years. DV's accounting policies are to revalue buildings every five years and depreciate them over their useful economic lives on the straight line basis. DV does not make an annual transfer from revaluation reserve to retained profits for excess depreciation.

DV received the following valuations from its professionally qualified external valuer:

| 31 August 20X1 | Building A | $180,000 |
| | Building B | $75,000 |

| 31 August 20X6 | Building A | $100,000 |
| | Building B | $30,000 |

249 Calculate the gain or impairment arising on the revaluation of Building A for the year ended 31 August 20X6.

$ _____. (Your answer should be rounded down to the nearest $)

250 Complete the sentence below by placing one of the following options into each of the spaces.

DV should _____ for the _____ on Building A for the year ended 31 August 20X6.

expense	impairment
reduce the revaluation reserve	revaluation
increase the revaluation reserve	

251 Calculate the gain or impairment arising on the revaluation of Building B for the year ended 31 August 20X6.

$ _____. (Your answer should be rounded down to the nearest $)

252 Complete the sentence below by placing one of the following options into each of the spaces.

DV should _____ for the _____ on Building B for the year ended 31 August 20X6.

expense to the profit or loss	impairment
reduce the revaluation reserve	revaluation
increase the revaluation reserve	

Data for Questions 253 and 254

Extracts from SF's statement of financial position at 31 March 20X3, with comparatives, are shown below:

	20X3	20X2
	$000	$000
Equity		
Ordinary shares	460	400
Share premium	82	70
Revaluation reserve	44	24
Retained earnings	273	246
Non-current liabilities		
Long term borrowings	129	105

During the year ended 31 March 20X3 SF's transactions included the following:

(i)   Repaid $25,000 of its long term borrowings during the year.

(ii)   Issued some ordinary shares at a 20% premium.

253 Calculate the proceeds from the share issue to be shown in the financing activities section of the statement of cash flow for the year ended 31 March 20X3, in accordance with IAS 7 Statement of Cash Flows.

$ _____. (Your answer should be rounded down to the nearest $)

254 What would be the entry shown for the loans to be shown in the financing activities section of the statement of cash flow for the year ended 31 March 20X3, in accordance with IAS 7 Statement of Cash Flows?

A   Net outflow of $24,000

B   Net inflow of $24,000

C   Outflow of $25,000 and inflow of $49,000

D   Outflow of $49,000 and inflow of $25,000

Data for Questions 255 and 256

AH owns three hotels. It has employed a firm of surveyors to revalue some of its properties during the past year. The directors have decided that the valuations should be incorporated into the entity's financial statements.

This is the first time that such a revaluation has taken place and the accountant responsible for the preparation of the non-current asset note in the statement of financial position is unsure of the correct treatment of the amounts involved. The entity's year end is 30 September 20X4.

The accountant has extracted the following table from the report prepared by the surveyors:

	Original cost	Depreciation to 30 September 20X3	Market value at 1 January 20X4
	$000	$000	$000
Hotel G	400	96	650
Hotel H	750	56	820
Hotel K	500	70	320

---

255 The carrying value of Hotel K has fallen as a result of the revaluation. How should this decrease be reflected in the financial statements?

A   The impairment of $110,000 should be debited to the statement of profit or loss

B   The impairment of $110,000 should be credited to the statement of profit or loss

C   The impairment of $110,000 should be credited to the revaluation reserve

D   The impairment of $110,000 should be debited to the revaluation reserve

256 What would be the balance on the revaluation reserve at 30 September 20X4?

A $362,000

B $472,000

C $140,000

D $320,000

257 **Complete the sentence below by placing one of the following options into each of the spaces. The options can be used more than once and not all options have to be used.**

A discontinued operation is a component of an entity that either has been disposed of or is classified as held for sale, and that represents a separate major line of _____ or _____ of operations that is part of a single co-ordinated plan to dispose of a separate major line of _____ or _____ of operations, or _____.

business	revenue
products or services	geographical area

Data for Questions 258 to 262

The financial statements of GK for the year to 31 October 20X8 were as follows:

Statement of financial positions at	31 October 20X8		31 October 20X7	
	$000	$000	$000	$000
Assets				
Non-current tangible assets				
Property	10,000		10,500	
Plant and equipment	5,000		4,550	
		15,000		15,050
Current assets				
Inventory	1,750		1,500	
Trade receivables	1,050		900	
Cash and cash equivalents	310		150	
		3,110		2,550
Total assets		18,110		17,600
Equity and liabilities				
Ordinary shares @ $0.50 each	6,000		3,000	
Share premium	2,500		1,000	
Revaluation reserve	3,000		3,000	
Retained earnings	1,701		1,000	
		13,201		8,000
Non-current liabilities				
Interest bearing borrowings	2,400		7,000	
		2,400		7,000

Statement of financial positions at	31 October 20X8		31 October 20X7	
	$000	$000	$000	$000
Current liabilities				
Trade and other payables	1,060		1,400	
Tax payable	1,449		1,200	
		2,509		2,600
		18,110		17,600

Statement of profit or loss for the year to 31 October 20X8

	$000	$000
Revenue		16,000
Cost of sales		10,000
Gross profit		6,000
Administrative expenses	(2,000)	
Distribution costs	(1,200)	(3,200)
		2,800
Finance cost		(600)
Profit before tax		2,200
Income tax expense		(999)
Profit for the period		1,201

Additional information:

1 Trade and other payables comprise:

	31 October 20X8	31 October 20X7
	$000	$000
Trade payables	730	800
Interest payable	330	600
	1,060	1,400

2 Plant disposed of in the year had a carrying amount of $35,000; cash received on disposal was $60,000.

3 GK's statement of profit or loss includes depreciation for the year of $1,110,000 for properties and $882,000 for plant and equipment.

4 Dividends paid during the year were $500,000.

258 Place the following options into the highlighted boxes in the table below to correctly calculate the cash generated from operations in accordance with the indirect method IAS 7 Statement of Cash Flows. The options cannot be used more than once and not all options have to be used.

600	(600)	150	(150)	4,297
1,992	(1,992)	70	(70)	4,347
25	(25)	60	(60)	3,245
250	(250)	35	(35)	3,295

GK's statement of cash flow YE 31 October 20X8	$000
Profit before tax	2,200
Finance cost	
Depreciation	
Gain on disposal of assets	
Inventory	
Receivables	
Payables	
	———
Cash generated from operations	
	———

259 What would be the tax paid amount for the year ended 31 October 20X8?

   A $999,000

   B $1,449,000

   C $249,000

   D $750,000

260 What would be the interest paid amount for the year ended 31 October 20X8?

   A $600,000

   B $870,000

   C $330,000

   D $270,000

261 Calculate the purchases of property, plant and equipment to be shown in the investing activities section of the statement of cash flow for the year ended 31 October 20X8, in accordance with IAS 7 Statement of Cash Flows.

   $ _____. (Your answer should be rounded down to the nearest $)

262 Calculate the cash flow from financing activities sections of GK's Statement of cash flows for the year ended 31 October 20X8, in accordance with IAS 7 Statement of Cash Flows.

   $ _____. (Your answer should be rounded down to the nearest $)

263 **Which THREE of the following are the main benefits, to users of the accounts, of including a statement of cash flows in published financial statements?**

    A   It can help users assess the liquidity and solvency of an entity

    B   It can help to identify the financial position of the entity

    C   It can help highlight where cash is being generated and where it is being spent

    D   It helps users assess financial adaptability

    E   It can help to identify the financial performance of the entity

    F   It helps to show inflows and outflows in three sections

Data for Questions 264 to 268

BI owns a building which it uses as its offices, warehouse and garage. The land is carried as a separate non-current tangible asset at the reporting date.

BI has a policy of regularly revaluing its non-current tangible assets. The original cost of the building in October 20X2 was $1,000,000; it was assumed to have a remaining useful life of 20 years at that date, with no residual value. The building was revalued on 30 September 20X4 by a professional valuer at $1,800,000.

BI also owns a brand name which it acquired 1 October 20X0 for $500,000. The brand name is being amortised over 10 years.

The economic climate had deteriorated during 20X5, causing BI to carry out an impairment review of its assets at 30 September 20X5. BI's building was valued at a market value of $1,500,000 on 30 September 20X5 by an independent valuer. A brand specialist valued BI's brand name at market value of $230,000 on the same date.

BI's management accountant calculated that the brand name's value in use at 30 September 20X5 was $150,000.

264 **What value should BI show the brand as in the statement of financial position for the year ended 30 September 20X5?**

    A $250,000

    B $200,000

    C $230,000

    D $150,000

265 **What amount should be credited to the revaluation reserve on 30 September 20X4 for the revaluation of the building?**

    A $800,000

    B $900,000

    C $950,000

    D $850,000

266 **Calculate the depreciation charge for the building for the year ended 30 September 20X5.**

    $ _____. (Your answer should be rounded down to the nearest $)

267 **Which of the following statements explains the treatment of the revaluation of the building on 30 September 20X5?**

    A   Debit the revaluation reserve with $300,000

    B   Debit the statement of profit or loss with $300,000

    C   Debit the revaluation reserve with $200,000

    D   Debit the statement of profit or loss with $200,000

268 **Calculate the depreciation charge for the building for the year ended 30 September 20X6.**

    $ _____. (Your answer should be rounded down to the nearest $)

269 **According to IAS 20 Accounting for Government Grants and Disclosure of Government Assistance, a revenue grant should only be recognised when:**

    A   the grant has been received

    B   the conditions of the grant have been complied with

    C   the entity has reasonable assurance they will receive the grant and comply with the conditions of the grant

    D   the entity has received the grant and the conditions of the grant have already been complied with

270 **According to IAS 20 Accounting for Government Grants and Disclosure of Government Assistance, how should revenue grants be accounted for?**

    A   Presented as a credit in the statement of profit or loss

    B   Presented as a credit in the statement of profit or loss, or deducted from the related expense

    C   Deducted from the related expense in the statement of profit or loss

    D   Credited to the statement of financial position as deferred income

271 **According to IAS 20 Accounting for Government Grants and Disclosure of Government Assistance, which TWO of the following statements explain how a capital grant can be accounted for?**

    A   Presented as a credit in the statement of profit or loss

    B   Presented as a credit in the statement of profit or loss, or deducted from the related expense

    C   Deducted from the related expense in the statement of profit or loss

    D   Deducted against the cost of the non-current asset

    E   Treat the grant as a deferred credit and transfer a portion to other income in the statement of profit or loss each year

272 An entity opens a new factory and receives a government grant of $30,000 in respect of capital equipment costing $200,000. It depreciates all plant and machinery at 20% pa straight-line.

Place the following options into the highlighted boxes in the table below to correctly show the treatment of the government grant for the first year using the deferral method. The options can be used more than once and not all options have to be used.

30,000	136,000	18,000
160,000	24,000	40,000
0	6,000	34,000

	Statement of profit or loss $		Statement of financial position $
Depreciation		Non-current asset	
Grant income		Government grant current liability	
		Government grant non-current liability	

273 An entity opens a new factory and receives a government grant of $30,000 in respect of capital equipment costing $200,000. It depreciates all plant and machinery at 20% pa straight-line.

Place the following options into the highlighted boxes in the table below to correctly show the treatment of the government grant for the first year using the deduction from the asset method. The options can be used more than once and not all options have to be used.

30,000	136,000	18,000
160,000	24,000	40,000
0	6,000	34,000

	Statement of profit or loss $		Statement of financial position $
Depreciation		Non-current asset	
Grant income		Government grant current liability	
		Government grant non-current liability	

274 An entity has a balance on the deferred income account of $15,000 relating to the balance of a grant given to them in order to produce 200 extra jobs. Due to a downturn in the economic climate the entity only managed to produce 50 extra jobs and the government asks for a repayment of $21,000. The original grant was issued at $45,000.

Place the following options into the highlighted boxes in the table below to correctly show the treatment of the repayment of the government grant. The options can be used more than once and not all options have to be used.

Debit	Statement of profit or loss	6,000
Credit	Bank	36,000
21,000	Deferred income	15,000
45,000	Non-current asset	4,000

		$

275 **Complete the sentence below by placing one of the following options into the space.**

IAS 40 Investment Property defines an investment property as _____.

land or a buildings originally acquired to earn rentals, but maybe used by the entity in the ordinary course of business
land or a buildings held to earn rentals, or for capital appreciation or both, rather than for use in the entity or for sale by the entity in the ordinary course of business for a period of less than 12 months
land or a buildings held to earn rentals, or for capital appreciation or both, rather than for use in the entity or for sale by the entity in the ordinary course of business

Data for Questions 276 and 277

An entity based in the US sells goods to the UK for £400,000 on 2 February 20X3 when the exchange rate was $/£0.65 (that is $1 = £0.65).

The customer pays in April 20X3 when the rate was $/£0.60 (that is $1 = £0.60).

276 **How does the entity account for the sale at 2 February 20X3?**

A	Debit receivables	$240,000	Credit sales	$240,000
B	Debit receivables	$666,667	Credit sales	$666,667
C	Debit receivables	$260,000	Credit sales	$260,000
D	Debit receivables	$615,385	Credit sales	$615,385

277 **What is the gain or loss on exchange when the payment is made in April 20X3?**

A   Gain of $51,282

B   Loss of $51,282

C   Gain of $20,000

D   Loss of $20,000

278 Complete the sentence below by placing one of the following options into each of the spaces.

IAS 21 The Effects of Changes in Foreign Exchange Rates states unsettled _____ items at the reporting date must be _____ and unsettled _____ items are _____.

monetary
non-monetary
retranslated using the closing rate
left at historical rate

Data for Questions 279 to 281

A US entity sells chairs to an entity based in Moldovia where the currency is the Moldovian pound (Mol). The chairs were sold on 1 October 20X1 for Mol 200,000 and were paid for in February 20X2.

The rate on 1 October 20X1 is US$/Mol 1.65 (that is $1 = Mol 1.65).

The rate on 31 December 20X1 (the reporting date) is US$/Mol 1.86 (that is $1 = Mol 1.86).

The rate on 4 February 20X2 is US$/1.91 (that is $1 = Mol 1.91).

---

279 How does the US entity account record the initial transaction?

A	Debit receivables	$121,212	Credit sales	$121,212
B	Debit receivables	$330,000	Credit sales	$330,000
C	Debit receivables	$107,527	Credit sales	$107,527
D	Debit receivables	$372,000	Credit sales	$372,000

280 How does the US entity account for the transaction in its financial statements for the year ended 31 December 20X1?

A   No additional adjustments required

B	Debit receivables	$13,685	Credit profit on exchange	$13,685
C	Debit loss on exchange	$13,685	Credit receivables	$13,685
D	Debit sales	$13,685	Credit receivables	$13,685

281 What is the gain or loss on exchange when the payment is made in February 20X2?

A   Gain of $2,815

B   Loss of $2,815

C   Gain of $16,500

D   Loss of $16,500

282 **Place the following options into the highlighted boxes in the table below to correctly show the characteristics of defined benefit and defined contribution scheme.**

The employer has an ongoing obligation to make sufficient contributions to the plan to fund the pensions
The employer undertakes to finance a pension income of a certain amount, e.g. 2/3 × final salary × (years of service/40 years)
The employer's contribution is usually a fixed percentage of the employee's salary
The annual cost to the employer is reasonably predictable
The cost of providing pensions is not certain and varies from year to year
The employer has no further obligation after a fixed amount is paid

	Defined contribution	Defined benefit
Characteristic		
Characteristic		
Characteristic		

Data for Questions 283 and 284

An entity makes contributions to a defined contribution pension fund for employees at a rate of 3% of gross salary. The contributions made are $8,000 per month for convenience with the balance being contributed in the first month of the following accounting year. The wages and salaries for 20X6 are $3.5m

283 **Calculate the pension expense for to be charged to the statement of profit or loss for 20X6.**

$ _____. (Your answer should be rounded down to the nearest $)

284 **Calculate the pension accrual/prepayment at the end of the year.**

$ _____. (Your answer should be rounded down to the nearest $)

285 **Complete the sentence below by placing one of the following options into each of the spaces.**

When an entity has a defined benefit pension scheme it recognises the net defined benefit liability (or asset) in the statement of financial position. If the plan has a liability it is measured at the _____ of the defined benefit obligation and if the plan has an asset it is measured at the _____ at the reporting date.

fair value
cost
present value
net realisable value

286 Place the following options into the highlighted boxes in the table below to correctly show the treatment of the following entries that will be required when an entity operates a defined benefit scheme.

| Current and past service costs |
| Interest cost (on liability) |
| Interest income (on asset) |

Statement of profit or loss (debit)	Statement of profit or loss (credit)	Statement of financial position (debit asset)	Statement of financial position (credit liability)

Data for Questions 287 and 288

An entity has a defined benefit pension plan and makes up financial statements to 31 March each year. The net pension liability (i.e. obligation less plan assets) at 31 March 20X3, was $52 million ($40 million at 31 March 20X2). The following additional information is relevant for the year ended 31 March 20X3:

- The discount rate relevant to the net liability at the start of the year was 10%.

- The current service cost was $35 million.

- At the end of the year the entity granted additional benefits to existing pensioners that have a present value of $12 million. These were not allowed for in the original actuarial assumptions.

- The entity paid pension contributions of $35 million.

---

287 Calculate the remeasurement component gains/losses arising in the year ended 31 March 20X3.

$ _____. (Your answer should be rounded down to the nearest $ million)

288 Calculate the total amount which has an effect on profit in the statement of profit or loss arising in the year ended 31 March 20X3.

$ _____. (Your answer should be rounded down to the nearest $ million)

289 At 1 January 20X4 Yogi acquired 100% of the share capital of Bear for $1,400,000. At 1 January 20X4 Yogi acquired 100% of the share capital of Bear for $1,400,000. At that date the share capital of Bear consisted of 600,000 ordinary shares of 50c each and its reserves were $50,000.

Goodwill impairment at 31 December 20X8 is assumed to be 60% of the goodwill at the date of acquisition.

In the consolidated statement of financial position of Yogi and its subsidiary Bear at 31 December 20X8, what amount should appear for goodwill?

A $420,000

B $630,000

C $300,000

D $450,000

290 At 1 January 20X8 Tom acquired 80% of the share capital of Jerry for $100,000. At that date the share capital of Jerry consisted of 50,000 ordinary shares of $1 each and its reserves were $30,000.

At 31 December 20X9 the reserves of Tom and Jerry were as follows:

Tom $400,000

Jerry $ 50,000

Goodwill impairment at 31 December 20X9 is assumed to be 60% of the goodwill at the date of acquisition. NCI is valued using the proportion of net assets method.

In the consolidated statement of financial position of Tom and its subsidiary Jerry at 31 December 20X9, what amount should appear for reserves?

A $428,400

B $416,000

C $394,400

D $398,720

291 At 1 January 20X6 Fred acquired 60% of the share capital of Barney for $750,000. At that date the share capital of Barney consisted of 20,000 ordinary shares of $1 each and its reserves were $10,000.

Goodwill impairment at 31 December 20X9 is valued at 20% of the goodwill at the date of acquisition. NCI is valued using the proportion of net assets method.

In the consolidated statement of financial position of Fred and its subsidiary Barney at 31 December 20X9, what amount should appear for goodwill?

A $146,400

B $732,000

C $576,000

D $585,600

292 At 1 January 20X6 Gary acquired 90% of the share capital of Barlow for $35,000. At that date the share capital of Barlow consisted of 20,000 ordinary shares of $1 each and its reserves were $10,000.

At 31 December 20X9 the reserves of Gary and Barlow were as follows:

Gary $40,000

Barlow $15,000

Goodwill impairment at 31 December 20X9 is valued at 20% of the goodwill at the date of acquisition. NCI is valued using the fair value method and valued at $4,000.

In the consolidated statement of financial position of Gary and its subsidiary Barlow at 31 December 20X9, what amount should appear for reserves?

A $42,880

B $44,500

C $43,060

D $42,900

293 At 1 January 20X8 Williams acquired 75% of the share capital of Barlow for $300,000. At that date the share capital of Barlow consisted of 400,000 ordinary shares of 50c each and its reserves were $60,000.

At 31 December 20X9 the reserves of Williams and Barlow were as follows:

Williams $200,000

Barlow $75,000

Goodwill impairment at 31 December 20X9 is valued at 20% of the goodwill at the date of acquisition. NCI is valued using the proportion of net assets method. In the consolidated statement of financial position of Williams and its subsidiary Barlow at 31 December 20X9, what amount should appear for goodwill?

Calculate the goodwill at 31 December 20X9.

$ _____. (Your answer should be rounded down to the nearest $)

294 HA acquired 80% of SB's equity shares on 1 April 20X0 for $185,000. The values of SB's equity at 1 April 20X0 was:

	$
$1 equity shares	150,000
Share premium	15,000
Retained earnings	(22,000)

NCI is valued using the proportion of net assets method.

Calculate the NCI arising on the acquisition of SB.

$ _____. (Your answer should be rounded down to the nearest $)

295 The HC group acquired 30% of the equity share capital of AF on 1 April 20X8 paying $25,000.

At 1 April 20X8 the equity of AF comprised:

	$
$1 equity shares	50,000
Share premium	12,500
Retained earnings	10,000

AF made a profit for the year to 31 March 20X9 (prior to dividend distribution) of $6,500 and paid a dividend of $3,500 to its equity shareholders.

Calculate the value of HC's investment in AF for inclusion in HC's statement of financial position at 31 March 20X9.

$ _____. (Your answer should be rounded down to the nearest $.)

296 HB sold goods to S2, its 100% owned subsidiary, on 1 November 20X8. The goods were sold to S2 for $33,000. HB made a profit of 25% on the original cost of the goods.

At the year-end, 31 March 20X9, 50% of the goods had been sold by S2. The remaining goods were included in inventory.

Which of the following statements explain the correct treatment for the adjustment required to inventory in the consolidated statement of financial position at 31 March 20X9?

A   Reduce inventory by $3,300   Increase cost of sales by $3,300

B   Increase inventory by $3,300   Reduce cost of sales by $3,300

C   Reduce inventory by $6,600   Increase cost of sales by $6,600

D   Reduce inventory by $4,125   Increase cost of sales by $4,125

Data for Questions 297 and 298

Stress acquired 80% of the ordinary share capital of Full on 1 October 20X7 when Full's retained earnings stood at $300,000. Full's statement of financial position at 30 September 20X9 is as follows:

	$000
Non-current assets	
Property, plant and equipment	1,800
Current assets	1,000
	–––––
	2,800
	–––––
Equity and reserves	
Share capital	1,600
Retained earnings	500
Current liabilities	700
	–––––
	2,800
	–––––

Stress has retained earnings of $1,500,000 at 30 September 20X9. NCI is valued using the proportion of net assets method.

---

297 **What is the retained earnings amount that will appear on the consolidated statement of financial position at 30 September 20X9?**

A $1,660,000

B $1,700,000

C $2,000,000

D $1,900,000

298 What is the NCI amount that will appear on the consolidated statement of financial position at 30 September 20X9?

    A $560,000

    B $100,000

    C $60,000

    D $420,000

299 During the year Fluff sold $168,000 worth of goods to its 90% owned subsidiary Ball. These goods were sold at a mark-up of 50% on cost. On 31 December Ball still had $36,000 worth of these goods in inventory.

What TWO statements calculate the PUP adjustment and explain the correct treatment in the consolidated statements?

    A   PUP is $56,000

    B   PUP is $12,000

    C   PUP is $18,000

    D   Reduce inventory and increase cost of sales

    E   Reduce inventory and reduce cost of sales

Data for Questions 300 to 303

Hard acquired 75% of the ordinary share capital of Work on 1 April 20X8. The summarised statement of profit or loss for the year-ended 31 March 20X9 is as follows:

	Hard	Work
	$000	$000
Revenue	120,000	48,000
Cost of sales	84,000	40,000
Gross profit	36,000	8,000
Distribution costs	5,000	100
Administration expenses	7,000	300
Profit from operations	24,000	7,600
Investment income	150	–
Finance costs	–	400
Profit before tax	24,150	7200
Tax	6,000	1,200
Profit for the year	18,150	6,000

During the year Work sold Hard some goods for $24m, these had originally cost $18m. At the year-end Hard had sold $20m (at cost to Hard) of these goods to third parties for $26m.

Goodwill impairment of $600,000 needs to be recorded for the current year and treated as an administration expense.

NCI is calculated using the fair value method.

300 Calculate the PUP adjustment for the year-ended 31 March 20X9.

$ _____. (Your answer should be rounded down to the nearest $)

301 What is the amount of profit attributable to the NCI for the year-ended 31 March 20X9?

A $1,100,000

B $1,500,000

C $1,250,000

D $1,350,000

302 What is the total amount for revenue and cost of sales to be shown in the consolidated statement of profit or loss for the year-ended 31 March 20X9?

	Revenue	Cost of sales
A	$144,000,000	$100,000,000
B	$168,000,000	$124,000,000
C	$192,000,000	$148,000,000
D	$144,000,000	$101,000,000

303 What is the total profit attributable to the parent to be shown in the consolidated statement of profit or loss?

A $24,150,000

B $22,550,000

C $21,450,000

D $30,000,000

Data for Questions 304 to 309

Really acquired 90% of the ordinary share capital of Hard on 1 January 20X9 when Hard had retained losses of $112,000 and 30% of the ordinary share capital of Work on 1 January 20X9 when Work had retained earnings of $280,000. The summarised statement of financial position for the year-ended 31 December 20X9 is as follows:

	Really $000	Hard $000	Work $000
Non-current assets			
Property, plant and equipment	1,918	1,960	1,680
Investment in Hard	1,610		
Investment in Work	448		
	3,976	1,960	1,680
Current assets			
Inventory	760	1,280	380
Receivables	380	620	200
Cash	70	116	92
	5,186	3,976	2352

	Really	Hard	Work
	$000	$000	$000
Equity and reserves			
$1 ordinary shares	2,240	1,680	1,120
Retained earnings	2,464	1,204	896
	4,704	2,884	2,016
Current liabilities			
Payables	300	960	272
Taxation	182	132	64
	5,186	3,976	2,352

An impairment test at year-end shows that goodwill for Hard remains unimpaired but the goodwill arising on the acquisition of Work has impaired by $5,600. NCI is valued using the proportion of net assets method.

304 **What is the total PPE amount to be shown in the consolidated statement of financial position?**

    A $3,878,000

    B $5,558,000

    C $3,682,000

    D $4,186,000

305 **Calculate the investment in associate amount to be shown in the consolidated statement of financial position.**

    $ _____. (Your answer should be rounded down to the nearest $)

306 **Complete the sentence below by placing one of the following options into the space.**

The goodwill amount to be shown in the consolidated statement of financial position is _____.

$nil	$(2,800)
$198,800	$42,000

307 **What is the total assets amount to be shown in the consolidated statement of financial position?**

    A $8,764,400

    B $7,930,000

    C $9,162,000

    D $9,470,000

308 **What is the total retained earnings amount to be shown in the consolidated statement of financial position?**

A $3,827,600

B $3,626,000

C $3,833,200

D $3,834,880

309 **Complete the sentence below by placing one of the following options into each of the spaces.**

The NCI amount to be shown in the consolidated statement of financial position is _____. NCI should be shown as _____.

$120,400	A non-current liability	$397,600
equity	$288,400	A current liability

310 HB paid $2.50 per share to acquire 90% of PN's equity shares on 1 September 20X8. At that date PN's statement of financial position showed the following balances with equity:

	$000
Equity shares of $1 each	180
Share premium	60
Retained earnings	40

NCI is valued using the fair value method. The fair value of NCI at acquisition was $60,000.

Calculate the goodwill arising on the acquisition of PN.

$ _____. (Your answer should be rounded down to the nearest $.)

311 **Place FOUR of the following options into the highlighted boxes in the table below to correctly show how goodwill should be recorded in the consolidated financial statements, in accordance with IFRS 3 Business Combinations. The options cannot be used more than once and not all options have to be used.**

Treat as an intangible asset
Expense to the statement of profit or loss
Not recognised in the financial statements
Amortise over its useful life
Undertake an impairment review each year
Not capable of a reliable measurement

Purchased goodwill	Internally generated goodwill

Data for Questions 312 to 314

HI, a parent entity, is planning to acquire a shareholding in ABC. The following alternative investment strategies are being considered:

(i)   HI can purchase 80,000 preferred shares in ABC

(ii)   HI can purchase 40,000 equity shares and 30,000 preferred shares in ABC

(iii)   HI can purchase 70,000 equity shares in ABC and no preferred shares.

ABC has the following issued share capital:

	$
$1 Equity shares	100,000
$1 10% Preferred Shares	100,000

Holders of preferred shares do not have any votes at annual general meetings.

312   Complete the sentence below by placing one of the following options into each of the spaces.

The acquisition of 80,000 preferred shares will _____ because the preferred shares _____. Therefore this investment would be classified as _____ in HI's financial statements.

not give control or any influence	a non-current investment
a subsidiary	give control and influence
are greater than 50%	an associate
have no voting rights	

313   Complete the sentence below by placing one of the following options into each of the spaces.

The acquisition of 40,000 equity shares and 30,000 preferred shares will give HI a _____ interest in ABC, this would be sufficient to give _____ of ABC. ABC would be classified as _____.

control	a subsidiary
40%	70%
significant influence	an associate

314   Complete the sentence below by placing one of the following options into each of the spaces.

The acquisition of _____ will give HI a 70% interest in ABC, this would be sufficient to give _____ of ABC. ABC would be classified as _____.

a subsidiary	an associate
significant influence	control
40,000 equity shares and 30,000 preferred shares	70,000 equity shares

315 On 1 April 20X3 JK acquired 100% of the equity shares of A and B as follows:

	$000	$000
	A	*B*
Cost of acquisition	850	610
Fair value of net assets at date of acquisition	750	500

At 31 March 20X4 IUJ carried out an impairment review of the goodwill arising on both acquisitions. At 31 March 20X4:

- the goodwill in A was NOT impaired but had actually increased in value by $40,000

- the goodwill in B had been impaired by $20,000

The total value of goodwill at 31 March 20X4 is:

A $210,000

B $230,000

C $190,000

D $250,000

316 **Complete the sentence below by placing one of the following options into each of the spaces.**

A subsidiary entity is an entity, including an unincorporated entity such as a partnership, which is controlled by another entity (known as the parent).

Control is the power to govern the financial and operating policies of an entity so as to obtain benefit from its activities. A controlling interest is usually obtained by acquiring more than _____.

An associated entity is an entity where another entity can exercise significant influence over the financial and operating policy decisions of that entity. Significant influence is not control over those policies. Significant influence is normally assumed to exist if an entity acquires _____.

25% or more of another entity's equity share capital	50% of the shares
20% or more of another entity's equity share capital	20% or more of another entity's share capital
50% of the equity shares	25% or more of another entity's share capital

317 An investment in another entity's equity is classified as an investment in a subsidiary, if the investor can exercise control over the investee.

AB acquired 4,000 of the 10,000 equity voting shares and 8,000 of the 10,000 non-voting preference shares of CD.

AB acquired 4,000 of the 10,000 equity voting shares of EF and had a signed agreement giving it the power to appoint or remove all of the directors of EF.

Place the following options into the highlighted boxes in the table below to correctly show how the investment in CD and EF should be treated. The options can be used more than once and not all options have to be used.

| Treat as a subsidiary |
| Treat as an associate |
| Exercises control of 40% |
| Exercises control of 60% |
| Has significant influence |
| Has effective control |

Investment in CD	Investment in EF

Data for Questions 318 to 320

YZ purchased 80% of the equity shares in WX on 1 October 20X2.

YZ and WX trade with each other. During the year ended 30 September 20X3 YZ sold WX inventory at a sales price of $28,000. YZ applied a mark-up on cost of 331/3%.

At 30 September 20X3 WX still owed YZ $10,000 of the cost and had remaining in inventory $6,000 of the goods purchased from YZ.

318 **What would be the journal entry to record the adjustment for the inter-company sale in the consolidated financial statements?**

   A   Debit revenue $28,000   Credit cost of sales $28,000

   B   Credit revenue $28,000   Debit cost of sales $28,000

   C   Debit revenue $10,000   Credit cost of sales $10,000

   D   Credit revenue $10,000   Debit cost of sales $10,000

319 **What would be the journal entry to record the adjustment for the inter-company balance in the consolidated financial statements?**

   A   Debit receivables $6,000   Credit payables $6,000

   B   Credit receivables $6,000   Debit payables $6,000

   C   Debit receivables $10,000   Credit payables $10,000

   D   Credit receivables $10,000   Debit payables $10,000

320 **What would be the journal entry to record the adjustment for the PUP in the consolidated financial statements?**

A	Debit inventory $1,500	Credit cost of sales $1,500
B	Credit inventory $1,500	Debit cost of sales $1,500
C	Debit inventory $2,000	Credit cost of sales $2,000
D	Credit inventory $2,000	Debit cost of sales $2,000

321 **AB owns 40% of CD. During the year the investment in CD suffered impairment of $1,000. How should the impairment be treated in the consolidated financial statements?**

A Increase the operating expenses by $1,000

B Reduce the share of the associates profit by $1,000

C Increase the operating expenses by $400

D Reduce the share of the associates profit by $400

MANAGEMENT OF WORKING CAPITAL, CASH AND SOURCES OF SHORT-TERM FINANCE

322 If an entity regularly fails to pay its suppliers by the normal due dates, it may lead to a number of problems:

(i) having insufficient cash to settle trade payables

(ii) difficulty in obtaining credit from new suppliers

(iii) reduction in credit rating

(iv) settlement of trade receivables may be delayed.

Which TWO of the above could arise as a result of exceeding suppliers' trade credit terms?

A (i) and (ii)

B (i) and (iii)

C (ii) and (iii)

D (iii) and (iv)

323 **A conservative policy for financing working capital is one where short-term finance is used to fund:**

A all of the fluctuating current assets, but no part of the permanent current assets

B all of the fluctuating current assets and part of the permanent current assets

C part of the fluctuating current assets and part of the permanent current assets

D part of the fluctuating current assets, but no part of the permanent current assets

324 ABC has produced the following sales forecast:

	$000
January	750
February	760
March	770
April	780
May	790
June	800

Currently 20% of customers pay in cash. Of the credit customers (excluding those who become irrecoverable debts), 60% pay in one month, 30% pay in two months and 10% in three months. Irrecoverable debts are 2%. This payment pattern is expected to continue.

Calculate the forecast cash receipts for April.

$ _____. (Your answer should be rounded down to the nearest $.)

325 **If the current ratio for a company is equal to its acid test (that is, the quick ratio), then:**

A   the current ratio must be greater than one

B   the entity does not carry any inventory

C   trade receivables plus cash is greater than trade payables minus inventory

D   working capital is positive

326 In October, a company made credit purchases of $18,000 and credit sales of $24,000. All sales are made on the basis of cost plus 25%.

Calculate how much the working capital will increase by in October as a result of these transactions.

$ _____. (Your answer should be rounded down to the nearest $)

327 **The following items have been extracted from an entity's budget for next month:**

	$
Sales on credit	240,000
Expected increase in inventory next month	20,000
Expected decrease in trade receivables next month	12,000

Calculate the budgeted receipt from trade receivables next month.

$ _____. (Your answer should be rounded down to the nearest $.)

328 DY had a balance outstanding on trade receivables at 30 September 20X6 of $68,000. Forecast credit sales for the next six months are $250,000 and customers are expected to return goods with a sales value of $2,500.

Based on past experience, within the next six months DY expects to collect $252,100 cash and to write off as irrecoverable debts 5% of the balance outstanding at 30 September 20X6.

Calculate DY's forecast trade receivables days outstanding at 31 March 20X7.

_____ days. (Your answer should be rounded down to the nearest day.)

329 A company has annual sales of $40 million, annual cost of sales of $30 million and makes annual purchases of $15 million. Its statement of financial position includes among assets and liabilities the following:

Trade receivables $4 million

Trade payables $3 million

Inventory $8 million

What is its working capital cycle?

A   206.5 days

B   60.8 days

C   36.5 days

D   97.3 days

330 XYZ's annual sales are $100m of which 95% are made on credit. Receivables at the beginning of the year were $10 million and at the end of the year total receivables were $12 million. 10% of receivables were non-trade related.

What is XYZ's average collection period?

A   36.5 days

B   40 days

C   38 days

D   46 days

331 DY's trade receivables balance at 1 April 20X6 was $22,000. DY's statement of profit or loss showed revenue from credit sales of $290,510 during the year ended 31 March 20X7.

DY's trade receivables at 31 March 20X7 were 49 days.

Assume DY's sales occur evenly throughout the year and that all balances outstanding at 1 April 20X6 have been received.

Also, it should be assumed all sales are on credit, there were no irrecoverable debts and no trade discount was given.

How much cash did DY receive from its customers during the year to 31 March 20X7?

A $268,510

B $273,510

C $312,510

D $351,510

332 The following items were extracted from an entity's budget for next month:

	$
Purchases on credit	360,000
Expected decrease in inventory during the month	12,000
Expected increase in trade payables during the month	15,000

Calculate the budgeted payment to trade creditors for the month.

$ _____. (Your answer should be rounded down to the nearest $)

333 The trial balance of EH at 31 October 20X7 showed trade receivables of $82,000 before adjustments.

On 1 November 20X7 EH discovered that one of its customers had ceased trading and was very unlikely to pay any of its outstanding balance of $12,250.

On the same date EH carried out an assessment of the collectability of its other trade receivable balances. Using its knowledge of its customers and past experience EH determined that the remaining trade receivables had suffered a 3% impairment at 31 October 20X7.

What is EH's balance of trade receivables, as at 31 October 20X7?

A $66,202

B $67,290

C $67,657

D $79,540

334 EV had inventory days outstanding of 60 days and trade payables outstanding of 50 days at 31 October 20X7.

EV's inventory balance at 1 November 20X6 was $56,000 and trade payables were $42,000 at that date.

EV's cost of goods sold comprises purchased goods cost only. During the year to 31 October 20X7, EV's cost of goods sold was $350,000.

Assume purchases and sales accrue evenly throughout the year and use a 365-day year. Further assume that there were no goods returned to suppliers and EV claimed no discounts.

Calculate how the amount EV paid to its credit suppliers during the year to 31 October 20X7.

$ _____. (Your answer should be rounded down to the nearest $)

335 DX had the following balances in its trial balance at 30 September 20X6:

Trial balance extract at 30 September 20X6

	$000	$000
Revenue		2,400
Cost of sales	1,400	
Inventories	360	
Trade receivables	290	
Trade payables		190
Cash and cash equivalents	95	

Calculate the length of DX's working capital cycle at 30 September 20X6.

_____ days. (Your answer should be rounded down to the nearest day.)

336 An entity commenced business on 1 April 20X2. Revenue in April 20X2 was $20,000, but this is expected to increase at 2% a month. Credit sales amount to 60% of total sales. The credit period allowed is one month. Irrecoverable debts are expected to be 3% of credit sales, but other customers are expected to pay on time. Cash sales represent the other 40% of revenue.

Calculate the cash expected to be received in May 20X2.

$ _____.(Your answer should be rounded down to the nearest $)

337 Which of the following is LEAST likely to characterise overtrading?

A   Increased borrowing

B   Increased cash balances

C   Increased turnover

D   Reduced working capital

338 Complete the sentence below by placing one of the following options into the space.

An aged trade creditor's analysis (aged trade payables analysis) is _____.

a listing of trade payables by date of invoicing
a listing of trade payables with whom you are in arrears
the proportion of purchases by value which are overdue
a breakdown of trade payables according to length of time elapsing since the purchase was made

339 Examine the validity of the following statements with respect to the Miller-Orr cash-management model.

Statement 1: The greater the variability in cash flows, the greater is the spread between the upper and lower cash balance limits.

Statement 2: The return point is the lower limit plus one-third of the spread.

	Statement 1	Statement 2
A	True	False
B	True	True
C	False	False
D	False	True

340 XYZ maintains a minimum cash holding of $10,000. The standard deviation of its daily cash flows is $4,000. The transaction cost per sale or purchase of marketable securities is $40. The daily interest rate is 0.04% per day.

Using the Miller-Orr cash management model, calculate the upper limit to the cash holdings of XYZ.

$ _____. (Your answer should be rounded to the nearest $1,000.)

Data for Questions 341 to 343

CT uses the Miller-Orr cash management model to help manage cash flows. The management accountant has agreed with the directors that the lower limit for cash will be $2,500.

The current rate of interest that CT pays is 0.025% per day. Each transaction costs CT $30. CT's daily cash flows have been measured and the variance calculated as $300,000.

341 Calculate for CT, the Miller-Orr spread.

$ _____. (Your answer should be rounded to the nearest $)

342 Calculate for CT, the Miller-Orr return point.

$ _____. (Your answer should be rounded to the nearest $)

343 Calculate for CT, the Miller-Orr upper limit.

$ _____. (Your answer should be rounded to the nearest $)

344 An entity uses the Baumol cash-management model. Cash disbursements are constant at $20,000 each month. Money on deposit earns 5% a year, while money in the current account earns a zero return. Switching costs (that is, for each purchase or sale of securities) are $30 for each transaction.

Calculate the optimal amount to be transferred in each transaction.

$ _____. (Your answer should be rounded to the nearest $100)

345 FGH requires a rate of return of 12.85% each year.

Two of FGH's suppliers, P and Q, are offering the following terms for immediate cash settlement:

Supplier	Cash settlement discount	Normal settlement period
P	1%	1 month
Q	2%	2 months

Which of the discounts should be accepted to achieve the required rate of return?

A   The discounts offered by both P and Q

B   The discount offered by P only

C   The discount offered by Q only

D   Neither of them

346 WM's major supplier, INT, supplies electrical tools and is one of the largest companies in the industry, with international operations. Deliveries from INT are currently made monthly, and are constant throughout the year. Delivery and invoicing both occur in the last week of each month.

Details of the credit terms offered by INT are as follows:

Normal credit period	*Cash discount*	*Average monthly purchases*
40 days	2% for settlement in 10 days	$100,000

WM always takes advantage of the cash discount from INT.

Calculate the annual rate of interest implied in the cash discount offered by INT. Assume a 365-day year.

_____ %. (Your answer should be rounded to two decimal places)

347 **What are the THREE main services provided by a without recourse factor?**

A   Sales ledger administration

B   Assistance in the creditworthiness of customers

C   Credit insurance

D   Advice on credit control policies

E   Factor finance

F   Training of sales ledger administration staff

348 **Complete the sentence below by placing one of the following options into the space.**

Invoice discounting normally involves _____.

offering a cash discount for early settlement of invoices

selling an invoice to a discount house at a profit

selling an individual invoice for cash to a factor organisation at a discount

writing off an invoice, partly or in total, as an irrecoverable debt

349 XYZ has $1 million to invest for one year. It can lock it away at a fixed rate of 7% for the full year, or invest at 6.5% for a three-month term, speculating on an increase in interest rates. Assume the rate available increases to 7.5% after three months and XYZ invests at this rate for the rest of the year.

By how much is XYZ better off from its gamble on interest rates?

A $2,500

B $12,836

C $73,414

D $3,414

350 After a bill of exchange has been accepted, there are a number of possible actions that the drawer could take.

Which of the following is NOT a possible course of action?

A   Ask the customer for immediate payment

B   Discount the bill with a bank

C   Hold the bill until the due date and then present it for payment

D   Use the bill to settle a trade payable

351 The bank accepts the instrument drawn upon it by its customer, and then sells it into a secondary market at a discount, including a commission, passing the proceeds to its client. The bank then pays the bill at face value.

Which description best describes this instrument?

A   A letter of credit

B   A forfaiting agreement

C   An acceptance credit

D   A commercial bill

352 **Which of the following most appropriately describes forfaiting?**

A   It is a method of providing medium-term export finance

B   It provides short-term finance for purchasing non-current assets which are denominated in a foreign currency

C   It provides long-term finance to importers

D   It is the forced surrender of a share due to the failure to make a payment on a partly paid share

353 Place THREE of the following options into the highlighted boxes in the table below to correctly show forms of short-term finance generally available to small entities.

Short-term government bonds
Interest bearing bank accounts
Trade payables
Negotiable instruments
Factoring
Invoice discounting

Forms of short-term finance

354 AL's customers all pay their accounts at the end of 30 days. To try and improve its cash flow, AL is considering offering all customers a 1.5% discount for payment within 14 days.

Calculate the implied annual (interest) cost to AL of offering the discount, using compound interest methodology and assuming a 365-day year.

_____ %. (Your answer should be rounded to one decimal place)

355 An entity's working capital financing policy is to finance working capital using short-term financing to fund all the fluctuating current assets as well as some of the permanent part of the current assets.

The above policy is an example of:

A   an aggressive policy

B   a conservative policy

C   a short-term policy

D   a moderate policy

356 BE has been offering 60-day payment terms to its customers, but now wants to improve its cash flow. BE is proposing to offer a 1.5% discount for payment within 20 days.

Assume a 365-day year and an invoice value of $1,000.

Calculate the effective annual interest rate that BE will incur for this action.

_____ %. (Your answer should be rounded to one decimal place)

357 The trade receivables ledger account for customer C shows the following entries:

		Debits	Credits
		$	$
Balance brought forward		0	
10 June X6	Invoice 201	345	
19 June X6	Invoice 225	520	
27 June X6	Invoice 241	150	
3 July X6	Receipt 1009 – Inv 201		200
10 July X6	Invoice 311	233	
4 August X6	Receipt 1122 – Inv 225		520
6 August X6	Invoice 392	197	
18 August X6	Invoice 420	231	
30 August X6	Receipt 1310 – Inv 311		233
7 September X6	Invoice 556	319	
21 September X6	Receipt 1501 – Inv 392		197
30 September X6	Balance	845	

Place FOUR of the following options into the highlighted boxes in the table below to correctly prepare an aged analysis showing the outstanding balance on a monthly basis for customer C at 30 September 20X6.

1,015	33	428	0
233	295	122	(325)
231	195	319	122

	Aged analysis
	$
June	
July	
August	
September	
	——
	845
	——

358 DR has the following balances under current assets and current liabilities:

Current assets	$
Inventory	50,000
Trade receivables	70,000
Bank	10,000

Current liabilities	$
Trade payables	88,000
Interest payable	7,000

DR's quick ratio is

A   0.80 : 1

B   0.84 : 1

C   1.47 : 1

D   1.37 : 1

359 SK sells bathroom fittings throughout the country in which it operates. In order to obtain the best price, it has decided to purchase all its annual demand of 10,000 shower units from a single supplier. RR has offered to provide the required number of showers each year under an exclusive long-term contract.

Demand for shower units is at a constant rate all year. The cost to SK of holding one shower unit in inventory for one year is $4 plus 3% of the purchase price.

RR is located only a few miles from the SK main showroom. It has offered to supply each shower unit at $400 with a transport charge of $200 per delivery. It has guaranteed such a regular and prompt delivery service that SK believes it will not be necessary to hold any safety inventory (that is, buffer inventory) if it uses RR as its supplier.

Using the economic order quantity model (EOQ model), calculate the optimal order size, assuming that RR is chosen as the sole supplier of shower units for SK.

_____ units. (Your answer should be rounded down to the nearest unit)

360   Which of the following would be LEAST likely to arise from the introduction of a Just-in-Time inventory ordering system?

A   Lower inventory holding costs

B   Less risk of inventory shortages

C   More frequent deliveries

D   Increased dependence on suppliers

361   Which of the following is LEAST relevant to the simple economic order quantity (EOQ) model for inventory?

A   Safety stock

B   Annual demand

C   Holding costs

D   Order costs

362   PB uses 2,500 units of component X per year. Its production director has calculated that the cost of placing and processing a purchase order for component X is $185, and the cost of holding one unit of component X for a year is $25.

What is the economic order quantity (EOQ) for component X and, assuming a 52-week year, what is the average frequency at which purchase orders should be placed?

	EOQ	Frequency of orders
A	136 units	3 weeks
B	136 units	6 weeks
C	192 units	4 weeks
D	192 units	5 weeks

363   Calculate the economic order quantity (EOQ) for the following item of inventory.

_____ units. (Your answer should be rounded up to the nearest unit)

• quantity required per year 32,000 items

• order costs are $15 per order

• inventory holding costs are estimated at 3% of inventory value per year

• each unit currently costs $40.

364 The economic order quantity formula includes the cost of placing an order. However, the Management Accountant is unsure which of the following items should be included in cost of placing an order.

Which THREE of the following would usually be regarded as part of the cost of placing an order?

A   Administrative costs

B   Postage

C   Quality control cost

D   Unit cost of products

E   Storekeeper's salary

F   Warehouse overheads

365 DS uses the Economic Order Quantity (EOQ) model. Demand for DS's product is 95,000 units per annum. Demand is evenly distributed throughout the year. The cost of placing an order is $15 and the cost of holding a unit of inventory for a year is $3.

Calculate how many orders DS should make in a year.

_____ orders. (Your answer should be rounded up to the nearest unit)

366 A bond with a coupon rate of 7% is redeemable in eight years' time for $100. Its current purchase price is $82.

Calculate the percentage yield to maturity.

_____ %. (Your answer should be rounded up one decimal place)

367 CX purchased $10,000 of unquoted bonds when they were issued by Z. CX now wishes to sell the bonds to B. The bonds have a coupon rate of 7% and will repay their face value at the end of five years. Similar bonds have a yield to maturity of 10%.

Calculate the current market price for the bonds.

$ _____. (Your answer should be rounded up to the nearest $)

368 A bond has a current market price of $83. It will repay its face value of $100 in 7 years' time and has a coupon rate of 4%.

If the bond is purchased at $83 and held, calculate its yield to maturity.

_____ %. (Your answer should be rounded to one decimal place)

369 DK is considering investing in government bonds. The current price of a $100 bond with 10 years to maturity is $88. The bonds have a coupon rate of 6% and repay face value of $100 at the end of the 10 years.

Calculate the yield to maturity.

_____ %. (Your answer should be rounded to two decimal places)

370 A bond has a coupon rate of 7%. It will repay its face value of $1,000 at the end of six years. The market expects this type of bond to have a yield to maturity of 10%.

Calculate the current market value for the bond.

$ _____. (Your answer should be rounded up to the nearest $)

Data for Questions 371 to 373

AM is a trading entity operating in a country where there is no sales tax. Purchases are on credit, with 70% paid in the month following the date of purchase and 30% paid in the month after that.

Sales are partly on credit and partly for cash. Customers who receive credit are given 30 days to pay. On average 60% pay within 30 days, 30% pay between 30 and 60 days and 5% pay between 60 and 90 days. The balance is written off as irrecoverable. Other overheads, including salaries, are paid within the month incurred.

AM plans to purchase new equipment at the end of June 20X5, the expected cost of which is $250,000. The equipment will be purchased on 30 days' credit, payable at the end of July.

The cash balance on 1 May 20X5 is $96,000.

The actual/budgeted balances for the six months to July 20X5 were:

All figures $000	Actual			Budgeted		
	Feb	Mar	Apr	May	Jun	Jul
Credit sales	100	100	110	110	120	120
Cash sales	30	30	35	35	40	40
Credit purchases	45	50	50	55	55	60
Other overhead expense	40	40	40	50	50	50

371 Place the following options into the highlighted boxes in the table below to correctly prepare the cash receipts budget for the period May to July 20X5. The options can be used more than once and not all options have to be used. (Round all figures to the nearest $000)

30	144	40	111
101	35	104	139
136	151	154	110

	May	June	July
	$000	$000	$000
Cash receipts			
Credit sale receipts			
	____	____	____
	____	____	____

372 Place the following options into the highlighted boxes in the table below to correctly prepare the purchase payments budget for the period May to July 20X5. The options can be used more than once and not all options have to be used. (Round all figures to the nearest $000)

54	59	55
65	50	58

	May	June	July
	$000	$000	$000
Credit purchase payments			

373 Place the following options into the highlighted boxes in the table below to correctly prepare a monthly cash budget for the period May to July 20X5. The options can be used more than once and not all options have to be used.

40	104	35	30	144	54	55
101	136	50	250	100	111	151
355	36	(204)	132	(32)	110	172

Cash budget	May	June	July
	$000	$000	$000
Cash sales			
Receipts from credit sales			
	——	——	——
Total receipts			
	——	——	——
Payments for purchases			
Expenses paid			
Equipment			
	——	——	——
Total payments			
	——	——	——
Net cash			
Balance b/f	96		
	——	——	——
Balance c/f			
	——	——	——

Data for Questions 374 and 375

DJ maintains a minimum cash holding of $1,000. The standard deviation of its daily cash flows has been measured at $300 (variance is $90,000). DJ's annual cash outgoings are $420,000 spread evenly over the year. The transaction cost of each sale or purchase of treasury bills is $25. The daily interest rate is 0.02% (7.3% per year).

374 **Using the Baumol cash management model, calculate the optimum amount of treasury bills to be sold each time cash is required.**

$ _____. (Your answer should be rounded up to the nearest $)

375 **Using the Miller-Orr cash management model, calculate the optimum amount of securities to sell when the cash holding reaches the lower limit.**

$ _____. (Your answer should be rounded up to the nearest $)

Data for Questions 376 and 377

DF is a manufacturer of sports equipment that has recently won a major three-year contract to supply FF with a range of equipment. FF is a large company with over 100 sports shops.

The new contract is expected to double DF's existing total annual sales, but demand from FF will vary considerably from month to month.

The contract will mean a significant additional investment in current assets. In particular, the contract with FF will require orders to be delivered within two days. This delivery period gives DF insufficient time to manufacture items, therefore significant inventories need to be held at all times. Also, FF requires 90 days' credit from its suppliers. This will result in a significant additional investment in receivables by DF.

If DF borrows from its bank to finance current assets, either using a loan or an overdraft, it expects to be charged annual interest at 12%. Consequently, DF is considering offering a 3% cash discount to FF for settlement within 10 days rather than the normal 90 days.

376 **Calculate the annual equivalent rate of interest implicit in offering a 3% cash discount to FF for settlement of debts within 10 days rather than 90 days.**

_____ %. (Your answer should be rounded up to one decimal place)

377 **Place FOUR of the following options into the highlighted boxes in the table below to correctly show which of the following would be factors, other than the rate of interest, which DF would need to consider before deciding on whether to offer a cash discount.**

Borrowing on overdraft might be more risky
It is cheaper to finance the higher receivables by borrowing than it would be to offer the cash settlement discount
The cash settlement discount arrangement may be difficult to withdraw at a future time, if DF no longer wants to offer it
Other customers might demand the same settlement discount terms as FF
It is more expensive to finance the higher receivables by borrowing than it would be to offer the cash settlement discount
Borrowing on overdraft might be less risky
The cash discount will be more flexible and easier to cancel if DF no longer wants to offer it

Factors to consider for offering a discount

378 Calculate the annual equivalent rate of interest implicit in offering a 2% cash discount to for settlement of debts within 10 days rather than 40 days.

Assume a 365-day year and an invoice value of $100.

_____ %. (Your answer should be rounded up to two decimal places)

379 SCL is a wholesale supplier of building materials. It is experiencing severe short-term cash flow difficulties. Sales invoices are about $2 million per month. The usual credit period extended to customers is 60 days, but the average period being taken is 90 days. The overdraft rate is 9% per annum.

A factoring company has offered a full factoring agreement without recourse on a permanent basis. The factor will charge a fee of 2.5% on total invoicing and will provide an immediate advance of 80% of invoiced amounts at an annual interest rate of 10%. Settlement of the remaining 20% will be after 60 days. SCL should avoid $300,000 a year in the administration costs of running the receivables ledger if the factoring arrangement is taken up.

Calculate the annual net cost, in cash terms, of the proposed factoring agreement assuming that there are 360 days in a year.

$ _____. (Your answer should be rounded to the nearest $)

380 FONT is a manufacturer of locks and household security fittings. Over the last 12 months it has encountered increasing problems with late payment by credit customers.

The last 12 months of credit sales of $67,500 show an increase of 10% over the previous year, but FONT's bank overdraft, on which it is charged interest at 9% per year, has also increased (by $1,800) over the last year. The management wants to reduce FONT's working capital requirements by reducing the trade receivables collection period.

The management accountant has extracted a profile of unpaid receivables (an 'aged debtors' profile) which is shown below:

% of total payments of trade receivables (by value)	Average collection period (days)
5	30
28	45
10	60
30	75
16	90
11	120

Irrecoverable debts currently stand at $2,000 per year.

FONT's management is considering whether to employ the services of a with recourse payments collection agency, which has quoted a fee of 1% of sales receipts. It is estimated that using the service will have the effect of reducing average days for credit customers to pay by 20 days and eliminating 50% of irrecoverable debts.

Calculate the net benefit or cost of using the factoring service.

$ _____. (Your answer should be rounded to the nearest $)

381 LOT produces garden seats which are sold on both domestic and export markets. Sales to the export market next year are expected to be $4.8 million, and are expected to occur steadily throughout the year. An initial deposit of 15% of the sales price is paid by all export customers.

All export sales are on 60 days' credit with an average collection period for credit sales of 75 days. Irrecoverable debts are currently 1.25% of export sales (net of the deposit).

LOT wishes to investigate the effects of extra advertising that could be undertaken to stimulate export sales. LOT has been approached by a European satellite TV company which believes that $300,000 of advertising could increase export sales in the coming year by up to 30%. There is a 0.2 chance of a 20% increase in export sales, a 0.5 chance of a 25% increase and a 0.3 chance of a 30% increase. Direct costs of production are 65% of the sales price. Administration costs would increase by $30,000, $40,000 and $50,000 for the 20%, 25% and 30% increases in export sales respectively. Increased export sales are likely to result in lengthening the average collection period of the credit element of all exports by five days, and irrecoverable debts will increase to 1.5% of all export credit sales.

LOT can borrow overdraft finance at 10% per year. These rates are not expected to change in the near future.

Place the following options into the highlighted boxes in the table below to correctly show the expected effect of the advertising campaign on the entity's annual profit.

2,016,000	504,000	2,100,000	(90,000)	(12,000)
336,000	2,184,000	(38,667)	(35,400)	(39,000)
(576,000)	(28,000)	(86,400)	(42,600)	(576,000)
(51,000)	420,000	(93,600)	(33,333)	
(624,000)	(15,000)	(600,000)	(18,000)	

	$	$	$
Extra contribution (35% × extra sales)			
Advertising costs	(300,000)	(300,000)	(300,000)
Extra administration costs	(30,000)	(40,000)	(50,000)
Increase in irrecoverable debts			
Extra cost of financing receivables (10% × extra receivables)			
	_____	_____	_____
Net effect on annual profit	(57,400)	7,667	72,733
	_____	_____	_____

382 The trade receivables ledger account for customer X is as follows:

		Debits	Credits	Balance
01 July	Balance b/fwd			162
12 July	Invoice AC34	172		334
14 July	Invoice AC112	213		547
28 July	Invoice AC215	196		743
08 August	Receipt RK 116 (Balance + AC34)		334	409
21 August	Invoice AC420	330		739
03 September	Receipt RL162 (AC215)		196	543
12 September	Credit note CN92 (AC112)		53	490
23 September	Invoice AC615	116		606
25 September	Invoice AC690	204		810
05 October	Receipt RM223 (AC420)		330	480
16 October	Invoice AC913	233		713
25 October	Receipt RM360 (AC615)		116	597

Place the following options into the highlighted boxes in the table below to correctly prepare an aged analysis showing the outstanding balance on a monthly basis for customer X at 31 October.

204	743	233	(4)
(213)	160	581	320
0	330	71	233

	Aged analysis
	$
July	
August	
September	
October	
	‾‾‾
	597
	‾‾‾

383 **Complete the sentence below by placing one of the following options into the space.**

An aged analysis of receivables allows an entity to _____.
It makes it more obvious whether an increase/decrease in a balance is due to changed activity levels or a change in payment policy by a customer. This makes it easier for the company to assess whether it should carry on doing business, how it should _____.
and whether it _____.

should offer discounts
set credit limits
focus its collection efforts to enforce its credit terms
see the total amount owed by customers
needs to take any action in respect of large balances
chase debts

Data for Questions 384 to 389

AD, a manufacturing entity, has the following balances at 30 April 20X5:

Extract from financial statements:	$000
Trade receivables	216
Trade payables	97
Revenue (all credit sales)	992
Cost of sales	898
Purchases (all credit purchases)	641
Inventories at 30 April 20X5:	
Raw materials	111
Work in progress	63
Finished goods	102

384   **Calculate AD's raw materials inventory days.**

_____ days. (Your answer should be rounded to the nearest day)

385   **Calculate AD's WIP inventory days.**

_____ days. (Your answer should be rounded to the nearest day)

386   **Calculate AD's finished goods inventory days.**

_____ days. (Your answer should be rounded to the nearest day)

387   **Calculate AD's receivables days.**

_____ days. (Your answer should be rounded to the nearest day)

388   **Calculate AD's payables days.**

_____ days. (Your answer should be rounded to the nearest day)

389   **Calculate AD's working capital cycle.**

_____ days. (Your answer should be rounded to the nearest day)

Data for Questions 390 and 391

BF manufactures a range of domestic appliances. Due to past delays in suppliers providing goods, BF has had to hold an inventory of raw materials, in order that the production could continue to operate smoothly. Due to recent improvements in supplier reliability, BF is re-examining its inventory holding policies and recalculating economic order quantities (EOQ).

- Item 'Z' costs BF $10.00 per unit.

- Expected annual production usage is 65,000 units.

- Procurement costs (cost of placing and processing one order) are $25.

- The cost of holding one unit for one year has been calculated as $3.

The supplier of item 'Z' has informed BF that if the order were 2,000 units or more at one time, a 2% discount would be given on the price of the goods.

390 Calculate the EOQ for item 'Z' before the quantity discount.

_____ units. (Your answer should be rounded to the nearest unit)

391 Calculate the total savings or cost of ordering 2,000 units instead of the EOQ to qualify for the 2% discount.

$ _____. (Your answer should be rounded to the nearest $)

392 DF, a sports and fitness training equipment wholesaler, has prepared its forecast cash flow for the next six months and has calculated that it will need $2 million additional short-term finance in three months' time.

DF has an annual gross revenue of $240 million and achieves a gross margin of 50%. It currently has the following outstanding working capital balances:

- $16 million trade payables, typical payables days for this industry is 45 days

- $20 million trade receivables, typical receivable days for this industry is 30 days

- $25 million bank overdraft.

DF forecasts that it will be able to repay half the $2 million within three months and the balance within a further three months.

Which THREE of the following are possible sources of short-term funding available to DF?

A Bank overdraft

B Factoring of receivables

C Increasing payables days

D Reducing receivables days

E Short-term loan

F Invoice discounting

393 ES estimates from its cash flow forecast that it will have $120,000 to invest for 12 months.

ES is considering the following investments:

(i) Purchase of fixed term bonds issued by a 'blue chip' entity quoted on the local stock exchange. The bonds have a maturity date in 12 months' time and pay 12.5% interest on face value. The bonds will be redeemed at face value in 12 months' time. ES will incur commission costs on purchasing the bonds of 1% of cost. The bonds are currently trading at $102 per $100

(ii) An internet bank is offering a deposit account that pays interest on a monthly basis at 0.8% per month.

Complete the sentence below by placing one of the following options into the space.

The most appropriate investment would be _____. _____ considered to be low risk.

| Both investments are |
| The bond is |
| The internet bank |
| The internet bank is |
| Purchase of the bonds |

394 **Which TWO correctly explain a coupon rate and the yield to maturity of a bond?**

A   The coupon rate is the interest rate payable on the amount paid for the bond

B   The yield to maturity is the effective yield on a redeemable security, taking into account both the interest yield and any gain or loss due to the fact that it was purchased at a price different to the redemption value

C   The coupon rate is the interest rate payable on the face (nominal) value of the bond

D   The yield to maturity is the effective yield on a redeemable security, taking into account the interest yield

E   The coupon rate is the interest payable upon redemption

395 BH purchased a bond with a face value of $1,000 on 1 June 20X3 for $850. The bond has a coupon rate of 7%. The bonds maturity date is 31 May 20X8 when it will be repaid at face value.

Calculate the bond's approximate yield to maturity.

_____ %. (Your answer should be rounded to the nearest whole figure)

396 **Place THREE of the following options into the highlighted boxes in the table below to correctly show forms of short-term investments generally available to small entities.**

Short-term government bonds
Interest bearing bank accounts
Trade payables
Negotiable instruments
Factoring
Invoice discounting

Forms of short-term investments

397 **Place the following options into the highlighted boxes in the table below to correctly show the advantages and disadvantages of using bank overdrafts and short-term bank loans.**

Generally more expensive	Repayable on demand
Fixed finance cost	Repayment date known
Flexible	Less flexible
Generally cheaper	Variable finance cost

	Bank overdrafts	Bank loans
Advantage		
Advantage		
Disadvantage		
Disadvantage		

398   Which TWO of the following are indicators of overtrading?

   A   A rapid decrease in current assets

   B   A rapid increase in turnover

   C   A rapid increase in liquidity ratios

   D   A rapid decrease in turnover

   E   A rapid increase in current assets

399   Which of the following does NOT influence the credit policy of an entity?

   A   Demand for products

   B   Profitability of products

   C   Competitor terms

   D   Risk of irrecoverable debts

400   Which of the following is an advantage of using a factoring agency for the collection of receivables?

   A   Customers will not know the debt has been sold to a factor

   B   Easy to change back to an internal debt collection system

   C   Cheaper than an internal debt collection system

   D   Savings on administration costs

401   Which of the following is an advantage of using an invoice discounting agency over a factoring agency?

   A   Invoice discounting is cheaper than factoring

   B   The debt collection is usually faster when using an invoice discounting agency

   C   The entity retains control over debt collection

   D   It is less risky than factoring

Section 2
ANSWERS TO OBJECTIVE TESTING QUESTIONS

FUNDAMENTALS OF BUSINESS TAX

1 The competent jurisdiction is **the country whose tax laws apply to the entity**.

2 A taxable person is **the person or entity who accountable for the tax payment.**

3 The answer is **A and B**.

4 **D**

5 Tax evasion is **an illegal way of avoiding paying taxes**, i.e. not declaring income or claiming false expenses.

6 **C**

7 A direct tax is one that **is levied directly on the person who is intended to pay the tax**.

8 **D**

9   B

The question says 'a dividend of $350,000 was paid' which implies this is the gross amount. Grossing up the $350,000 was not required as it was meant to be assumed that this was the gross figure. The answer was therefore calculated on the gross figure of $350,000 as follows:

	$
Tax on profits (25% × 750,000)	187,500
Shareholder:	
Dividend received	
Net – (350,000 × 75%)	262,500
Tax credit (262,500/75 × 25)	87,500
	————
Gross dividend	350,000
Tax @ 30%	105,000
Less tax credit	(87,500)
	————
Tax on dividend	17,500
	————
Total (187,500 + 17,500)	205,000

10   C

11   D

12   A

A tax authority is unlikely to have the power of arrest. This power will usually be restricted to the police or other law enforcement officers.

13   The answer is **A and D**.

The OECD's list of permanent establishments includes a place of management, a workshop and a quarry. A building site is only included if it lasts more than 12 months. Specifically excluded from the definition of permanent establishment are facilities used only for the purpose of storage, display or delivery of goods. A branch is considered as a permanent establishment not a subsidiary.

14   C

A = 17/75 = 22.7% tax paid on profits

B = 4.8/44 = 10.9% tax paid on profits

Therefore, the greater the profits, the greater the tax percentage, hence this is a progressive tax.

15   The answer is **A, E and F.**

B, C and D are possibly results of setting deadlines because if tax is paid on time it is likely it will cost less to collect it, therefore easier to administer and it is possible payments will be more accurate if the return is done sooner rather than later. However, these three are not the main reasons for setting deadlines.

16   **C**

Equity

17   The answer is **A, B and F.**

C is incorrect as although payments may be more accurate if the employer is using a software package to calculate the tax it is not necessary so. Self-assessment calculations should also be correctly calculated. D is incorrect as the employee has no cost of using the PAYE system and E is incorrect as this is a benefit to the employee and not the government.

18   From the revenue authority's point of view, a commodity is suitable for an excise duty to be imposed if:

Suitable for excise duties
There are few large producers/suppliers
Demand is inelastic with no close substitutes
Sales volumes are large

19   **B**

20   **A**

Hypothecation is the means of devoting certain types of expenditure for certain things, e.g. Road tax is used for maintaining roads.

21   **C**

22   The answer is **A and C.**

B, D and E are the same as income.

23   **C**

24   **A**

25   **A**

HD has the responsibility to pay the sales tax to the tax authorities and will have direct contact with them, therefore this is known as formal incidence.

26   **B**

27   B

28   The answer is **$3,133.**

DB – Corporate income tax 20X6

	$
Profit before tax per accounts	33,950
Add back:	
Entertaining	600
Local government tax	950
Depreciation on buildings	1,600
Depreciation on plant and equipment	20,000
	57,100
Less: tax depreciation	
Building (70,000 × 4%)	(2,800)
Plant and equipment (W1)	(25,768)
Taxable profit	28,532

			Tax $
Taxable at 15%	(25,000 – 10,000) =	15,000	2,250
Taxable at 25%	(28,532 – 25,000) =	3,532	883
Corporate income tax 20X6			3,133

(W1)

	Plant and equipment	New plant	Total
	$	$	$
Cost	80,000		
20X5 tax depreciation @ 27%	(21,600)		
	58,400		
20X6 tax depreciation @ 27%	(15,768)		15,768
Cost		20,000	
20X6 first year allowance @ 50%		(10,000)	10,000
	42,632	10,000	25,768

29 **D**

	$
Accounting profit	860,000
Add depreciation	42,000
Add amortisation	15,000
	917,000
Less tax depreciation	(51,000)
Taxable profit	866,000
Tax @ 25%	216,500

30 **D**

31 **D**

32 Under the OECD model tax convention an entity will generally have residence for tax purposes in **the country of its effective management.**

33 **B**

34

Powers of the tax authority
Power to exchange information with tax authorities in other jurisdictions
Power to review and query filed returns

35 **C**

36 **A**

37 **D**

38 Tax avoidance is **a legal way of avoiding taxes.** It is tax planning to arrange affairs, within the scope of the law, to minimise the tax liability.

39 **C**

Entities can use any rate for accounting depreciation, so to ensure that all entities are taxed equally the tax authority sets rates for tax depreciation for all entities. The tax depreciation rates then replace accounting depreciation in the tax computations and it can be greater or less depending on the tax rules in force in the country of residence.

40 **D**

41 The answer is **$2,837.**

FB – Corporate income tax

	$
Profit for the year	29,800
Add back:	
Depreciation building	3,200
Depreciation plant and equipment	6,000
Depreciation furniture and fittings	5,000
Less: Accounting gain on disposal	(4,000)
	40,000
Less: Tax depreciation	
FYA – plant and equipment ($30,000 × 50%)	(15,000)
Buildings ($80,000 × 5%)	(4,000)
Disposal balancing allowance	(6,812)
(Proceeds $5,000 – TWDV $11,812)	
Taxable profit	14,188
Tax at 20%	2,837

42 The answer is **$34,100.**

JW – Corporate income tax

	$
Accounting profit before tax	150,000
Add back:	
Entertaining	2,200
Depreciation on vehicle ($12,000/6)	2,000
Depreciation on plant and equipment	27,000
	181,200
Less: tax depreciation	
Plant and equipment	(40,000)
Vehicle ($12,000 × 40%)	(4,800)
Taxable profit	136,400
Tax at 25%	34,100

43   The answer is **$38,050.**

JW – Income tax expense

	$
Under-provision	3,950
Current tax charge (question 42)	34,100
Income tax expense	38,050

44   The answer is **$36,450.**

KM – Corporate income tax

	$
Profit before tax	165,000
Add back:	
Entertaining	9,800
Depreciation on vehicle ($18000/6)	3,000
Depreciation on plant and equipment	42,000
	219,800
Less: tax depreciation	
Plant and equipment	(65,000)
Vehicle ($18,000 × 50%)	(9,000)
Taxable profit	145,800
Tax at 25%	36,450

45   The answer is **$29,200.**

KM – Income tax expense

	$
Current tax charge (question 44)	36,450
Over-provision	(7,250)
Income tax expense	29,200

46   The answer is **$29,087.**

HG – Corporate income tax

	$
Profit before tax	167,000
Add back:	
Entertaining	4,000
Political donations	5,000
Accounting depreciation (50,000 + 8,000 = 58,000/5)	11,600
Less: non-taxable income	(12,000)
Less: tax depreciation (W1)	(10,250)
	165,350
Less: losses b/fwd	(49,000)
Taxable profit	116,350
Tax at 25%	29,087

(W1)

Tax depreciation:

	Plant and equipment	New plant	Total
	$	$	$
Cost	50,000		
20X1 tax depreciation @ 50%	(25,000)		
	25,000		
20X2 tax depreciation @ 25%	(6,250)		6,250
Cost		8,000	
20X2 first year allowance @ 50%		(4,000)	4,000
	18,750	4,000	10,250

47   **D**

Excise duties are placed on inelastic products not elastic.

48

Type of tax	Single stage	Multi-stage
Characteristic	Tax at one level of production	Tax at each level of production
Characteristic		This could be cascade tax
Characteristic		This could be VAT

49

Type of tax	Unit tax	Ad valorem tax
Characteristic	This is charged on weight or size	This is charged on the value of the units sold
Characteristic	Example WZ pays $1 per bottle sold	Example WZ sells for $8.05 inclusive of VAT at 15%

50 The answer is **A, C and D.**

B is incorrect because VAT will not be charged on all supplies, only taxable supplies and E is incorrect because VAT can only be recovered on purchases if the purchase is used to produce a taxable supply. F is incorrect as standard returns are made quarterly and not monthly.

51

Year	Taxable profits	Taxable gains
1	$ nil	$6,000
2	$ nil	$ nil
3	$ nil	$ nil
4	$60,000	$3,000

Year 1: No taxable trading profits and taxable capital gains of $6,000. $50,000 of the trading losses in Year 2 can be carried back and set off against the profit in Year 1, reducing the taxable trading profit to 0. The capital loss in Year 2 cannot be carried back to Year 1.

Year 2: No taxable trading profits or gains. Trading loss and capital loss in the year. Unrelieved trading losses of $40,000 and the unrelieved capital losses of $8,000 are carried forward to Year 3.

Year 3: No taxable trading profits or gains. Unrelieved trading losses of $40,000 are set against the trading profits of $30,000. The unrelieved trading loss is now $10,000 and is carried forward to Year 4. The unrelieved capital loss brought forward is set off against the capital gain in Year 3, leaving $3,000 of unrelieved capital losses to carry forward to Year 4.

Year 4: Taxable trading profits of $60,000 and taxable capital gains of $3,000. Taxable trading profits = $70,000 – $10,000 unrelieved losses brought forward. Taxable capital gains = $6,000 – $3,000 unrelieved losses brought forward.

52 **C**

Group loss relief allows members of the group to surrender their losses to any other member of the group. Consolidation of profits and losses does not apply to tax computations and so answer A is incorrect. Group loss relief is an option that can be taken by the group, and is not compulsory. Therefore answers B and D are incorrect.

53

Year	Corporate income tax due	Capital tax due
30 September 20X3	$40,000	$ nil
30 September 20X4	$ nil	$ nil
30 September 20X5	$6,000	$6,000

30 September 20X3   Trading profit $200,000 × 20% = $40,000

Capital loss c/f $100,000 so nil taxable

30 September 20X4   Trading loss c/f $120,000 so nil taxable

Capital loss of $100,000 b/f is c/f so nil taxable

30 September 20X5   Trading profit $150,000 − $120,000 = $30,000 × 20% = $6,000

Capital gain $130,000 − $100,000 = $30,000 × 20% = $6,000

54   The answer is **A and D.**

Relief can be claimed earlier because if the surrendering entity keeps the loss for their own use it will be carried forward for many years. The group company may pay tax at a higher rate, therefore more tax can be saved by reducing the taxable profit.

55   **A**

	$
Disposal proceeds	1,200,000
Selling costs	(9,000)
Net proceeds	1,191,000
Cost	(600,000)
Additional costs	(5,000)
	586,000
Indexation (605,000 × 60%)	(363,000)
Taxable gain	223,000
Tax @ 25%	55,750

56   The answer is **$41,400.**

		$
Disposal proceeds		1,250,000
Less: Costs of disposal		(2,000)
		1,248,000
Acquisition costs:		
Purchase cost	630,000	
Costs arising on purchase ($3,500 + $6,500)	10,000	
Renovation costs	100,000	
		(740,000)
Indexation – 50% × $740,000		(370,000)
Taxable gain		138,000
Tax @ 30%		41,400

57   The answer is **$42,625.**

	$
Disposal proceeds	1,200,000
Costs to sell	(17,000)
Net proceeds	1,183,000
Cost	(650,000)
Duties	(25,000)
	508,000
Indexation (675,000 × 50%)	(337,500)
Taxable gain	170,500
Tax @ 25%	42,625

58   The answer is **$12,000.**

	$
Disposal proceeds	450,000
Costs to sell	(15,000)
Net proceeds	435,000
Cost	(375,000)
Duties	(12,000)
Taxable gain	48,000
Tax @ 25%	12,000

59   D

The site of the 11 month construction contract is not a permanent establishment according to the OECD model because it is less 12 months.

60   B

An overseas branch is an extension of the main business activity and not treated as a separate entity for taxation purposes.

61   C

Withholding tax is a tax deducted at source before payment of interest or dividends.

62

Type of tax	Cascade tax	VAT
Characteristic	Multi-stage	Multi-stage
Characteristic	Tax at each level of production	Tax at each level of production
Characteristic	No refunds are provided by local government on purchase tax	Refunds are provided on purchase tax provided the purchases are used for a taxable supply

63   The answer is **$29,000.**

		$
Disposal proceeds		1,000,000
Less: Costs of disposal		(6,000)
		994,000
Acquisition costs:		
Purchase cost	850,000	
Costs arising on purchase ($5,000 + $8,000)	13,000	
Clearing land costs	15,000	
		(878,000)
Taxable gain		116,000
Tax @ 25%		29,000

64   Under the OECD model an entity will have residence **in the country of effective management.**

65   D

Each of the other three factors can be taken into account in determining tax residence.

66   C

Effective management and control is the over-riding test under the OECD model tax convention.

67   D

The tax deducted at source from the dividend in the foreign country prior to distribution to EB is called the withholding tax.

68   B

Double tax relief does not prevent you from paying tax twice. For example, suppose that your company is based in Country A and has a subsidiary operating in Country B, and there is a double taxation agreement between the countries. If tax on profits in Country B is 10% and in Country A is 15%, your company would pay tax at 10% in Country B and tax at 15% in Country A on the subsidiary's profits. Double tax relief therefore mitigates tax – you don't have to pay 35% in tax (10% + 25%) – but you might still have to pay tax on the profits twice, once in each country.

69   C

The country of control overrides the others for residency.

70   D

71   The answer is **A and B.**

72   D

73

MT – Corporate income tax	$
Accounting profit	37,000
Donations	$5,000
Accounting depreciation	$39,000
Tax depreciation	($45,000)
Tax losses	($12,000)
	————
Taxable profit	$24,000

*Note: Tax depreciation = (120,000 × 25%) + (30,000 × 50%) = $45,000

74

Type of supply	Zero rated	Exempt
Characteristic	Entity must register for VAT purposes	Entity does not register for VAT purposes
Characteristic	VAT can be claimed back on purchases	VAT cannot be claimed back on purchases

75 A capital gain is **the profit made on the disposal of a chargeable asset.**

76 A capital tax is **the tax charged on the profit made on the disposal of a chargeable asset.**

77 The answer is **$177,120.**

	$
Charge for year (946,000 × 22%) =	208,120
Over-provision from previous year	(31,000)
Income tax expense	177,120

78 A

	$
Current year charge	320,000
Over-provision for prior year (290,000 – 280,000)	(10,000)
Charge	310,000

79 A tax base represents **what is being taxed.**

80 The answer is **$17,500.**

(4/12 × $75,000 × 20%) + (8/12 × $75,000 × 25%)

81 The answer is **A, C and E.**

A tax base is something that is liable to tax, e.g. income or consumption of goods.

Tax bases regularly used by governments are:

- income – for example, income taxes and taxes on an entity's profits
- capital or wealth – for example, taxes on capital gains and taxes on inherited wealth
- consumption – for example, excise duties and sales taxes/VAT.

82 The answer is **$22,500.**

	$
Accounting profit	95,000
Adjustments:	
Non-taxable income	(15,000)
Non-tax allowable expenditure	10,000
Taxable profits	90,000
Tax at 25%	22,500

83 Benefits in kind represent **non-cash benefits given to an employee as part of their remuneration package.**

84 The answer is **$37,250.**

KQ – Corporate income tax

	$
Accounting profit	147,000
Adjustments:	
Add back: disallowed expenses (9,000 + 6,000)	15,000
Add back: accounting depreciation (180,000 + 50,000) × 15%	34,500
Less: tax depreciation (W1)	(47,500)
Taxable profits	149,000
Tax at 25%	37,250

(W1)

	$
Tax depreciation:	
First year allowance 50,000 × 50% =	25,000
Annual allowance (180,000 – 90,000 FYA 50% for 30/9/X1) × 25% =	22,500
Total tax depreciation	47,500

85 The answer is **A, B and D.**

Excise Duty is a selective commodity tax, levied on certain types of goods. It is a unit tax based on the weight or size of the tax base. E.g. Petroleum products, tobacco products alcoholic drinks and motor vehicles.

From the revenue authority's point of view, the characteristics of commodities that make them most suitable for excise duty to be applied are:

- Few large producers

- Inelastic demand with no close substitutes

- Large sales volumes

- Easy to define products covered by the duty

86 The answer is **$200,250.**

The accounting profit should be reported before recognising any dividends paid.

	$
Accounting profit	822,000
Add: Entertaining expenses	32,000
Donation to political party	50,000
Less: Government grant income	(103,000)
	801,000
Tax @ 25%	200,250

87

	Tax avoidance	Tax evasion
Characteristic	A legal way of reducing your tax bill	An illegal way of reducing your tax bill
Characteristic	For example AB invests surplus income into tax-free securities to avoid paying tax on the interest	For example AB does not declare his income from his night security job

88 B

89 C

90 D

91 B

92 D

93 The answer is **$35,250**.

	$
Disposal proceeds	210,000
Acquisition costs:	
Purchase cost	55,000
Costs arising on purchase	5,000
Indexation ($55,000 + $5,000) × 15%	9,000
	(69,000)
Taxable gain	141,000
Tax @ 25%	35,250

94 B

95 B

96 The answer is **$2,970.**

	$
Disposal proceeds	80,000
Costs to sell	(2,000)
Net proceeds	78,000
Acquisition costs:	

Purchase cost	50,000	
Import duties	8,000	
Indexation ($50,000 + $8,000) × 14%	8,120	
		(61,120)

Taxable gain	11,880
Tax @ 25%	2,970

97 **A**

	$
Disposal proceeds	110,000
Acquisition costs:	

Purchase cost	45,000	
Costs arising on purchase	5,000	
Indexation ($45,000 + $5,000) × 35%	17,500	
		(67,500)

Taxable gain	42,500
Tax @ 25%	10,625

98 An indexation allowance **reduces a chargeable gain.**

99 **B**

A = 15/75 = 20% tax paid on profits

B = 8/40 = 20% tax paid on profits

Therefore, the regardless of the profits, the tax percentage remains the same, hence this is a proportionate tax.

100

	Transfer pricing
Characteristic	This results in transactions not taking place at 'arm's length' and profits being effected by the group members
Characteristic	This arises in group situations when either goods are sold inter-company or a loans take place at a favourable price

REGULATORY ENVIRONMENT FOR FINANCIAL REPORTING AND CORPORATE GOVERNANCE

101 An asset is a **resource controlled by the entity as a result of past events and from which future economic benefits are expected to flow to the entity.**

102 B

The auditor expresses an opinion on the truth and fairness of the financial statements; the auditor does not certify that the financial statements give a true and fair view – statement (i) is therefore false. All the other statements are correct.

103 C

The disagreement is material and it affects the auditor's opinion. However, as the financial statements are not seriously misleading, the auditor should issue an 'except for' qualification. (If the financial statements were seriously misleading, he would issue an adverse opinion.)

104 The objective of financial reporting is **to provide information about the reporting entity that is useful to a wide range of users in making economic decisions.**

105 B

The other three are important concepts of accounting but only the going concern concept is highlighted as the underlying assumption in The Framework.

106 D

The IFRS Interpretations Committee interprets International Financial Reporting Standards and, after public consultation and reporting to the IASB, it issues an interpretation.

107 A

The IFRS Foundation is the supervisory body, and consists of trustees whose main responsibilities are governance issues and ensuring that sufficient funding is available.

108 The answer is **B and E.**

When there is a material misstatement in the external auditor's opinion (as distinct from a pervasive qualification) the audit report should a modified one with a qualified opinion. The auditors will state that, in their opinion, the financial statements give a true and fair view, except for....

109 B

The auditor has been prevented from obtaining sufficient appropriate audit evidence.

110 B

111

Powers of auditors
Power to access the books, records, documents and accounts
Power to attend and speak at meetings of equity holders
Power to require officers of the entity to provide them with information and explanations

112 The answer is **C and E.**

113 The elements are assets, liabilities, income, **expenses** and **equity.**

114 C

An auditor will give their opinion of whether the financial statements show a true and fair view and can suggest to the directors to change the statements but cannot correct the statements themselves.

115 A

116 The answer **is B, D and E.**

117 A

118 The IASB's Framework identifies two methods of capital maintenance which are the **financial** concept and the **physical** concept.

119 The IASB's Framework identifies the underlying assumption as the **going concern** concept.

120

The objective of an external audit
To see if the financial statements show a true and fair view
To see if the financial statements have been prepared in accordance with appropriate accounting standards

121 D

The objectives of financial statements are set out in the IASB Framework. Note that providing information about 'changes in the financial position', as well as information about financial position and financial performance, is included in these objectives.

122 B

You should learn the IASB definitions of both assets and liabilities. The definition in the question is in two parts: (1) a liability is a present obligation that has arisen out of a past event, and (2) it is certain or probable that settlement of this obligation will result in an outflow of economic benefits, such as a payment of money. It is also necessary for the amount of the liability to be measured reliably.

123 C

The IASB Framework states that materiality is a threshold or cut-off point for reporting information, but is not a qualitative characteristic that financial information must have to be useful.

124 Expenses are **decreases in economic benefits during the accounting period in the form of outflows or depletions of assets that result in decreases in equity, other than those relating to distributions to equity participants.**

125 A

126 The answer is **A and E.**

127 C

The IASB Framework defines equity as the residual interest in the assets of the enterprise after all the liabilities have been deducted from total assets. It is important to recognise this idea that equity is a balancing figure: Assets – Liabilities. Statements of financial position should be prepared with a view to measuring assets and liabilities in the best manner, and equity is the amount left over when liabilities are subtracted from assets.

128 D

129 A

130 D

E stands to make a gain if he manipulates the figures to get a better bonus, hence E is in a position of a self-interest threat.

131

Factors influencing accounting and disclosure
Social
Economic
Political

132 B

133 D

134 C

135

Functions of the IFRS Advisory Council
To give advice to the IASB on agenda decisions
To give advice to the IASB on the priorities in its work
To give any other advice to the IASB or the Trustees

136 The TWO fundamental qualitative characteristics are **relevance** and **faithful representation.**

137 Item (iv) of the report is **opinion.**

138 **D**

139 **A**

140 **D**

141 The answer is **B and C.**

142

	Adopting International Financial Reporting Standards (IFRS) as its local standards	Modelling local accounting standards on the IASB's IFRSs, but amending them to reflect local needs and conditions	Develop its own accounting standards with little or no reference to IFRSs
Advantage	Quick to implement	Standards should be more relevant to local needs and compliant with International Standards	Any standards developed will be specific to C's requirements
Disadvantage	Standards may not take into account any specific local traditions or variations	It will take longer to implement and requires an adequate level of expertise to exist within the country	It will not be quick to implement

143

The purpose of the Framework
Assist users of financial statements that are prepared using IFRSs
Assist the IASB in the development of future IFRSs and in its review of existing IFRSs
Assist auditors in forming an opinion as to whether financial statements conform with IFRSs

144 **A**

As the directors refuse to amend the valuation of inventory and inventory amount is material ($1m = 25% of profit) but not pervasive (only inventory is a problem – not the whole accounts) a modified audit report should be issued.

The modified report should have a qualified opinion because we have a material misstatement in the accounts. This means the auditors would say something like…. "the accounts show a true and fair view, except on the valuation of inventory…..".

145

Principle-based accounting standards	Prescriptive accounting standards
The standard would be applied using professional judgement	The standard would require a certain treatment to be used, regardless of the situation
Flexible	Less flexible
Standards should ensure the spirit of the regulations are adhered to	Standards more likely to lead to the letter of the law being followed rather than the spirit

146 Income is **increases in economic benefits during the accounting period in the form of inflows or enhancements of assets; or decreases of liabilities that result in increases in equity, other than those relating to combinations from equity participants.**

147 The Framework criteria states:

- it is **probable** that any future economic benefit associated with the item will flow to or from the entity; and

- the item has a cost or value that can be measured **with reliability**.

148 The answer is **A and D.**

According to CIMA's Code of ethics for professional accountants CX is in a position where she may be compromising her integrity and objectivity.

Integrity – This principle imposes an obligation to be truthful and honest on the accountant. A professional accountant should not be associated with reports or other information where she/he believes that the information contains misleading statements. This seems to be the case with the revised forecasts; CX believes that the revised forecasts are 'grossly overstated'.

Objectivity – A professional accountant should not allow conflict of interest or undue influence of others to override professional or business judgements or to compromise their professional judgements. The management board are overriding CX's professional and business judgement as they are imposing their assumptions on the forecast profits.

149

	Dealing with an ethical dilemma
1	Gather evidence and document the problem
2	Report internally to immediate management
3	Report internally to higher management
4	Report externally
5	Remove herself from the situation

150

Report	Opinion
Modified	Qualified

The research cost should be expensed to the statement of profit or loss and NOT capitalised as per IAS 38. The mistake is material but not material and pervasive, hence a qualified opinion.

151 The answer is **C and E.**

152 The answer is **A and D.**

RS must also comply with the CIMA codes fundamental principles of integrity and objectivity. Changing the management information would breach both of these principles.

153 **D**

154

IFRS Foundation	International Accounting Standards Board (IASB)	IFRS Advisory Council	IFRS Interpretations Committee
Governance and fund raising	Responsibility for all technical matters including the preparation and publication of international financial reporting standards	Provides strategic advice to the IASB and informs the IASB of public views on major standard setting projects	Provides timely guidance on the application and interpretation of IFRSs

155 The answer **is A, C and D.**

The ethical problem that XQ faces is that a professional accountant in business should prepare or present information fairly, honestly and in accordance with relevant professional standards so that the information will be understood in its context. A professional accountant is expected to act with integrity and objectivity and not allow any undue influence from others to override his professional judgement.

XQ is facing pressure from others to change the results and therefore break the CIMA Code.

XQ is being asked to misrepresent the facts of the actual situation which would be contrary to the CIMA Code's fundamental principles of integrity and objectivity. XQ would also be breaking the due care requirement of the CIMA Code.

156 **C**

157 The answer is **A and E.**

An external audit does not make the financial statements error free, just free of material misstatements. The auditor will review the financial statements and advise on changes, they do not prepare the financial statements.

158 **C**

He should start by gathering all relevant information so that he can be sure of the facts and decide if there really is an ethical problem. All steps taken should be fully documented.

Initially he should raise his concern internally, possibly with the team's manager or a trusted colleague.

If this is not a realistic option, for example because of the relationship of the manager and the team member that Ace is concerned about, he may have to consider escalating the issue and speak to the manager's boss, a board member or a non-executive director. If there is an internal whistle blowing procedure or internal grievance procedure he should use that.

If after raising the matter internally nothing is done and he still has concerns he should take it further, for example if the other team member is an accountant Ace could consider reporting the team member to his professional body.

Ace could also distance himself from the problem and ask to be moved to a different department or to a different team.

159 **A**

160 **C**

161 **D**

162 **C**

163

Fundamental	Enhancing
Relevance	Comparability
Faithful representation	Timeliness
	Understandability
	Verifiability

164 **A**

165 **C**

166 **B**

167 The purpose of corporate governance is to protect the **shareholders.**

168 Corporate governance is the means by which a company is **operated** and **controlled**.

169 **D**

170

Rules-based	Principle-based
Applied in the US	Applied in the UK
Instils the code into law	Comply with the code or explain why
Penalties for transgression	Adhere to the spirit rather than the letter of the code

FINANCIAL ACCOUNTING AND REPORTING

171 The answer is **$13,778.**

The calculation is as follows:

	$000
Profit before tax	12,044
Add Depreciation	1,796
Loss on sale of tangible non-current assets	12
	13,852
Increase in inventories	(398)
Increase in receivables	(144)
Increase in payables	468
Cash generated from operations	13,778

172 The answer is **$105,000.**

	$000
Balance at 30 September 20X4	180
Revaluation (30 – 10)	20
Disposal at CA (90 – 85)	(5)
Depreciation	(40)
	——
	155
Balance at 30 September 20X5	(260)
	——
Purchases	105
	——

Disposal

	$000		$000
Cost	90	Bank	15
Profit	10	Dep'n (balance)	85
	——		——
	100		100
	——		——

173 **A**

	$
Accrued interest b/f	12,000
Interest payable per statement of profit or loss	41,000
Accrued interest c/f	(15,000)
	————
Paid	38,000
	————

174 The answer is **$350,000.**

	$000
Total opening balance	460
Add: Tax charge for the year	450
	——
	910
Less: Total closing balance	(560)
	——
Tax paid during the period	350
	——

175 A

Tax creditor			
		B/f	133
Paid	98	Statement of profit or loss	122
C/f	157		
	255		255

176 The answer is **A and E.**

177 The answer is **A, C and E.**

178 D

179 A

180 B

181 An operating segment is defined by IFRS 8 as a component of an entity whose **operating** results are regularly reviewed by the entity's chief operating **decision maker** to make decisions about resources to be allocated to the segment and assess its **performance**.

182 C

The prior period error is corrected by restating the comparative amounts for the previous period at their correct value. A note to the accounts should disclose the nature of the error, together with other details.

183 A

B and D are examples of changes in estimates and C is an example of a change in policy.

184

Change in policy
Required by a new or revised accounting standard
Results in financial statements will provide more reliable and more relevant information

185 B

A change from capitalising a cost to treating it as a revenue expense would be classified as a change in accounting policy under IAS 8.

186 The answer is **D and E.**

Items A, B and C are examples of changes in estimates.

187 D

Items A and B are a change in policy and item C is an error.

188 The answer is **$3,640.**

	$
Cost	100,000
Depreciation 31/3/X3	(25,000)
	75,000
Depreciation 31/3/X4	(18,750)
	56,250
Depreciation 31/3/X5	(14,063)
	42,187
Depreciation 31/3/X6	(10,547)
	31,640
Recoverable amount	(28,000)
Impairment loss	3,640

189 The answer is **$580,000.**

	Land	Buildings	Total
	$000	$000	$000
Cost	120	200	
Accumulated depreciation to the revaluation date	–	(100)	
Carrying value at the revaluation date	120	100	220
Revalued amount	200	600	800
Credit to revaluation reserve			580

190 The answer is **$60,000.**

The building will be depreciated over its remaining expected useful economic life, which is 10 years. The annual depreciation charge for the building will therefore be $600,000/10 years = $60,000 each year.

191 C

The four definitions might all seem similar, but property, plant and equipment are **tangible** assets, not any assets. IAS 16 states that a tangible asset should be held for **more than one accounting period** (rather than for more than 12 months) to qualify as property, plant and equipment.

192 The answer is **$129,000.**

	$
Cost of basic machine	100,000
Special modifications made to basic design	15,000
Supplier's engineer's time installing and initial testing of machine	2,000
Concrete base	12,000
	129,000

We do not include the three year maintenance cost as this is not a one off cost and would be expensed to the statement of profit or loss.

JT can reclaim back VAT hence would not form part of the cost of non-current assets.

193 A

IAS 16 states that when the revaluation model is used, revaluations should be made with sufficient regularity to ensure that the carrying value of the assets remain close to fair value. IAS 16 also states that, if one item in a class of assets is revalued, all the assets in that class must be revalued.

194 The answer is **A and D.**

			$
1 July 20X2	Cost		50,000
30 June 20X3	Carrying amount	80% × 50,000	40,000
30 June 20X4	Carrying amount	60% × 50,000	30,000

On 1 July 20X4 the asset is revalued from a carrying amount of $30,000 to a fair value of $60,000, establishing a revaluation reserve of $30,000. There are three years of useful life remaining.

		$
30 June 20X5	Carrying amount = ⅔ × 60,000	40,000
1 July 20X5	Disposal proceeds	35,000
Loss on disposal		(5,000)

There is a loss on disposal of $5,000, and the $30,000 revaluation reserve is transferred to retained earnings as a movement on reserves.

195 A

As the lining of the furnace was identified as a separate item in the accounting records, its replacement will be viewed as capital expenditure. The other three options all involve either replacing part of an asset or restoring it to its original condition.

196 The answer is **$5,250 pa.**

	$
1.10.X2 purchase	21,000
Depreciation to 30.9.X5	
21,000/6 × 3	(10,500)
Balance 30.9.X5	10,500

The machine will be used for two more years, at which point it will be worthless. Assuming that production is still profitable with the increased depreciation charge, it should be written off over its remaining useful life, such that the charge recognised in the year to 30 September 20X6 should be $5,250 ($10,500 × ½).

197 The answer is **$66,500.**

Workings:

	$
Cost 1/4/X1	100,000
$100,000/10 × 2 years	(20,000)
Carrying amount 31/03/X3	80,000
To revaluation reserve	15,000
Revaluation (1/4/X3)	95,000
Depreciation $95,000/8 years	(11,875)
B/f 1/4/X4	83,125
Depreciation $83,125/5 years	(16,625)
Carrying amount at 31/3/X5	66,500

198 **D**

The allocation of EW's administration costs would not be included as these costs are not directly incurred as a result of carrying out the construction.

199 **C**

The asset was previously revalued by $200,000, therefore when it is devalued by $250,000 the reserve is removed and the balance charged to the statement of profit or loss.

200 B

The cost of the decommissioning is assumed to be an obligation for the company. If so, an amount should be included in the cost of the asset when it is first recognised (on 1 July 20X4).

The amount to include in the cost of the asset for decommissioning costs is the present value of the expected future decommissioning costs. The present value is calculated by multiplying the expected future cost by a discount factor, which in this case is the discount factor for Year 5 (20X9) at 12%. $4,000,000 × 0.567 = $2.268 million.

Therefore:

Debit: Cost of asset $2.268 million
Credit: Provision for decommissioning costs $2.268 million

The asset is depreciated in the normal way, which in this example is on a straight-line basis over five years.

In addition, the decommissioning cost should be increased to $4 million by the end of Year 5. This is done by making a finance charge each year. This is charged at the cost of capital (12%) and applied to the balance on the provision account. The finance charge for the year to 30 June 20X5 is 12% × $2.268 million = $272,160.

Debit: Finance charge (expense) $272,160
Credit: Provision for decommissioning costs $272,160

	$
Depreciation charge ($2.268 million/5 years)	453,600
Finance charge	272,160
	————
Impairment loss	725,760
	————

201   The answer is **A and E.**

	Land $ million	Buildings $ million	Total $ million
At 30 June 20X5			
Carrying amount	1.00	4.80	5.80
Building depreciation = $5 million/50 years = $100,000 per year			
Revalued amount	1.24	5.76	7.00
			————
Transfer to revaluation reserve			1.20
			————
At 30 June 20X7			
Carrying amount	1.24	5.52	6.76
Building depreciation = $5.76 million/48 years = $120,000 per year			
Disposal value			6.80
			————
Gain on disposal			0.04

The gain on disposal is $40,000. The $1.2 million balance on the revaluation reserve is transferred from the revaluation reserve to retained earnings in the SOCIE but is not reported through the statement of profit or loss for the year.

202 A

Research costs are expensed to the statement of profit or loss as per IAS 38.

203 The answer is **$8,912.**

	$
Carrying amount at the time of the impairment review ($76,000 × 80% × 80% × 80%)	38,912
Revised carrying amount after impairment review	30,000
Impairment (charge in the statement of profit or loss)	8,912

Note: The revised carrying amount (recoverable amount), is the higher of value in use $30,000 or fair value less costs to sell $27,000.

204 B

The answer is **$80,000.**

An asset should be valued at the lower of carrying amount and recoverable amount. Recoverable amount is the higher of (a) fair value less costs to sell and (b) value in use.

	A	B	C
Carrying amount	200	300	240
Recoverable amount	240	260	200
Impairment loss	nil	40	40

80

205

Treatment of publishing rights
The rights do not meet the definition of an asset as we do not have a reliable cost
Expense the rights to the statement of profit or loss at $100,000

The rights do not meet the definition of an asset. As a gift they do not have a cost and there is no reliable measurement of probable future benefit.

206 The answer **is $130,000.**

Goodwill is the remaining balance after the fair value of the net tangible assets acquired and the other intangible assets acquired have been subtracted from the total purchase consideration.

	$	$
Purchase price		
Shares (10,000 × $20)		200,000
Cash		20,000
		220,000
Assets acquired		
Net tangible non-current assets	25,000	
Patents	15,000	
Brand name	50,000	
		90,000
Value of goodwill		130,000

207

IAS 38's criteria for recognition
An intention to complete the project
An ability to use or sell the developed item
The developed item with generate a probable future economic benefit

Although the other three items are similar to the criteria they are not specific, i.e. costs must be measured reliably, not just measured. You must have adequate cash to complete the project but you must also have other resources. The criteria of the standard states adequate resources in general, not just adequate cash.

208 A

When purchased goodwill is reduced in value due to impairment, the impairment loss should be reported through the statement of profit or loss as a loss for the period, and should not be taken directly to reserves.

209 The answer is **$200,000.**

Expenditures on the project during the year to 31 December 20X1 are research costs, which are charged as an expense in the statement of profit or loss for the year.

Expenditure in the year to 31 December 20X2 ($1,000,000) should be capitalised and reported in the statement of financial position at the year end. All the expenditure should be capitalised, because the recoverable amount of the expected future benefits exceeds the costs incurred.

In the year to 31 December 20X3, the expenditures should again be included in development costs as a non-tangible asset. However, at the end of the year, the accumulated expenditures capitalised are $2,200,000 ($1,000,000 + $1,200,000). This exceeds the recoverable amount of $2,000,000.

For the year to 31 December 20X3, an impairment cost of $200,000 should therefore be charged in the statement of profit or loss.

The value of the development costs in the statement of financial position at 31 December 20X3 is $2,000,000.

210   D

Item A cannot be capitalised because it does not meet all the criteria, i.e. it is not viable.

Item B is research and cannot be capitalised.

Item C cannot be capitalised because it does not meet all the criteria, i.e. making a loss.

211   C

The recoverable amount of an asset is the higher of (a) fair value less costs to sell ($18,000) and (b) value in use ($22,000).

212

Property, plant and equipment note 31 December 20X5

	Land	Buildings	Plant and machinery	Under construction	Total
Cost/valuation	$000	$000	$000	$000	$000
Balance at 1 January 20X5	2,743	3,177	1,538	53	7,511
Revaluation of assets	375	–	–	0	375
Disposal of assets	–	–	(125)	–	(125)
Transfers	–	–	350	(350)	0
Additions	402	526	890	297	2,115
Balance at 31 December 20X5	3,520	3,703	2,653	0	9,876
Depreciation					
Balance at 1 January 20X5	–	612	671	–	1,283
Disposal of assets	–	–	(111)	–	(111)
Depreciation for the year	–	75	212	–	287
Balance at 31 December 20X5	0	687	772	0	1,459
Carrying amount 31 December 20X5	3,520	3,016	1,881	0	8,417
Carrying amount 31 December 20X4	2,743	2,565	867	53	6,228

213 The answer is **$55,800.**

	Cost	Recoverable amount (Net Realisable Value)	Lower of cost and recoverable amount
Item 1	$24,000	See note 1	$24,000
Item 2	$33,600	$31,800 (note 2)	$31,800
			$55,800

Notes:

1   The recoverable amount is not known, but it must be above cost because the contract is expected to produce a high profit margin. The subsequent fall in the cost price to $20,000 is irrelevant for the inventory valuation.

2   The recoverable amount is $36,000 minus 50% of $8,400.

214 The answer is **B, D and E.**

IAS 2 states that:

(a)   selling costs cannot be included in inventory cost, therefore A cannot be included

(b)   general overheads cannot be included C

(c)   overhead costs should be added to inventory cost on the basis of normal capacity of the production facilities, therefore F cannot be included in cost

(d)   the cost of factory management and administration can be included, so that item D can be included in inventory values.

215 D

The fire is an example of a non-adjusting event as it arose after the reporting date and does not provide evidence of a condition that existed at the reporting date.

216 C

The warehouse fire is an adjusting event as it occurred before the reporting date. Settlement of the insurance claim should therefore be included in the financial statements. The other events are non-adjusting as they occurred after the reporting date and do not provide evidence of conditions existing at the reporting date.

217 The answer is **C and E.**

The share issue takes place after the reporting date is not an adjusting event. Plans to acquire another entity after the reporting date are not adjusting events.

218 B

219 The answer is **D and E.**

Dividends declared after the reporting date but before the accounts are signed are not provided for but should be disclosed by way of note.

The dividend is shown as a deduction in the statement of changes in equity for the year in which it is actually paid.

220

Adjusting events	Non-adjusting events
One month after the reporting date a court determined a case against XS and awarded damages of $50,000 to one of XS's customers. XS had expected to lose the case and had set up a provision of $30,000 at the reporting date	A month after the reporting date XS's directors decided to cease production of one of its three product lines and to close the production facility
One month after the year end XS's main customer goes into liquidation owing XS a substantial amount of money	A dispute with workers caused all production to cease six weeks after the reporting date
XS discovers a material error in the closing inventory value one month after the reporting date	Three weeks after the reporting date a fire destroyed XS's main warehouse facility and most of its inventory

221 The answer is **$3,700,000.**

The division is presumably a cash-generating unit that will be classified as a discontinued operation within the meaning of IFRS 5. A discontinued operation is one that has been disposed of or is classified as 'held for sale'.

IFRS 5 requires that assets (or a group of assets) classified as held for sale should be measured at the lower of carrying amount and fair value less costs to sell. This means that any future profits on disposal cannot be recognised (since carrying amount is lower).

IFRS 5 also requires that on the face of the statement of profit or loss there should be a total figure for:

(a)   the post-tax profit or loss of the discontinued operation, and

(b)   the post-tax gain or loss recognised on the measurement to fair value less costs to sell of the assets constituting the discontinued operation.

This total figure should also be analysed into its component elements (either in a note to the accounts or on the face of the statement of profit or loss).

The total figure to be shown for the year is therefore:

	$
Profit from discontinued operation	300,000
Item (i): Provision for closure costs	(3,000,000)
Item (iii): Impairment of plant	(1,000,000)
Amount to disclose for the discontinued operation	(3,700,000)

Notes:

1   The closure costs should not include any apportionment of head office costs.

2   It is assumed that the loss on the sale of the plant in January gives evidence of an impairment in value, which is therefore included as an adjusting event after the reporting date.

3   We could also argue the gain of $2,000,000 could also be included as it is certain to happen, however, has been excluded from the answer under prudence. We do not normally recognise income until it is virtually certain.

222   A

223   The answer is **B and D.**

Expenses are analysed into cost of sales, distribution costs and administrative expenses.

224   The answer is **$688,000.**

Cost of sales	$
Trial balance	480,000
Depreciation (1,500 – 540) × 20%	192,000
Inventory adjustment *	16,000
	688,000

***Note:** The inventory is valued at lower of cost or NRV, hence must be reduced by $16. By reducing the closing inventory value it will have the impact of increasing cost of sales.

225   The answer is **$760,000.**

Administrative	$
Trial balance	260,000
Provision	500,000
	760,000

226   The answer is **$220,000.**

The finance cost represents the interest due for the year and not paid, i.e. $2,200,000 × 10%.

227   C

Both items must be shown on the face of the statement of profit or loss. Other items to include in the statement of profit or loss include revenue, the tax expense and the profit or loss for the period (IAS 1).

228 A

IAS 1 states that the financial statements must be prepared on a going concern basis, unless management intends to liquidate the entity or to cease trading, or has no realistic alternative but to do so. When the financial statements are not prepared on a going concern basis, this fact must be disclosed. It is not therefore a requirement of IAS 1 that a note should state that the accounts are prepared on a going concern basis. (However, there might be a similar requirement, for example in a corporate governance code, that the directors should state in the annual report and accounts that the entity is a going concern.)

229 The answer is **B and D.**

Revenue and finance costs must be shown on the face of the statement of profit or loss.

230 A

A revaluation of a non-current asset is not reported through the statement of profit or loss, but as an adjustment to the equity reserves (revaluation reserve account). The revaluation will therefore affect the statement of financial position and the statement of changes in equity, but not the statement of profit or loss. A revaluation is not a cash flow transaction, and so would not appear in the statement of cash flows.

231 The answer is **$440,000.**

Workings:

	$000
Opening balance	45
Sales for the year	445
Closing balance	(50)
	____
Cash received from customers	440
	____

232 The answer is **$225,000.**

	$000
Opening balance	20
Purchases (see below)	235
Closing balance	(30)
	____
Cash paid to suppliers	225
	____
Purchases =	
Cost of material used	220
Closing inventory	40
Opening inventory	(25)
	____
	235
	____

233

FC's statement of cash flow YE 31 March 20X8	$000
Profit before tax	133
Finance cost	20
Depreciation	92
Gain on disposal of assets	(60)
Inventory	(15)
Receivables	(5)
Payables	10
	────
Cash generated from operations	175
	────

234 The answer is **C and D.**

At the date when an asset meets the criteria as an asset held for sale it should be shown separately on the statement of financial position and depreciation should cease.

235 The answer is **A and D.**

According to CIMA's Code of ethics for professional accountants WZ is in a position where he may be compromising his integrity and objectivity.

Integrity – This principle imposes an obligation to be truthful and honest on the accountant. A professional accountant should not be associated with reports and other information where she/he believes that the information contains misleading statements. This seems to be the case with the revised treatment of the property, WZ believes that the revised financial statements will not follow IFRS 5 and may not show a true and fair view of the situation.

Objectivity – A professional accountant should not allow conflict of interest or undue influence of others to override professional or business judgements or to compromise her/his professional judgements. The management board is overriding WZ's professional and business judgement as it is imposing its business judgement over the professional accountant's (WZ) professional judgement.

236

	Change in useful life of an asset
Characteristic	A change in useful life is treated as a change in estimate as per IAS 8 Accounting Policies, Changes in Accounting Estimates and Errors
Characteristic	Depreciation charge for 31 March 20X3 should be $2,500

A requirement of IAS 16 Property, Plant and Equipment is that the useful economic life (and the residual value) of each item of property, plant and equipment should be reviewed at least once each year. If there is a change in the estimate, a change in accounting estimate should be made in accordance with IAS 8 Accounting Policies, Changes in Accounting Estimates and Errors.

The delivery vehicle is currently valued at cost less accumulated depreciation. At 1 April 20X2, the asset had been held for two years, and its expected useful life was four years. Its carrying amount was therefore $10,000, which is $20,000 cost less two years of accumulated depreciation of $5,000 per year.

At 31 March 20X3, the revision to the estimated useful life means that from 1 April 20X2, the asset had four more years of expected useful life. From that date, the asset should therefore be depreciated over its remaining revised expected useful life. The annual depreciation charge from 1 April 20X2 should therefore be $2,500 (= $10,000/4 years).

This means that for the year to 31 March 20X3, the annual depreciation charge should be $2,500. The carrying amount of the asset at the beginning of the year, as indicated above, is $10,000. The carrying amount at 31 March 20X3 will be:

	$
Vehicle at cost	20,000
Less accumulated depreciation	12,500
Carrying amount	7,500

237 CD should **capitalise** the development costs and they should be shown as an **intangible asset** on the **statement of financial position**.

As all of the IAS 38 criteria seem to have been met by CD's new process CD will treat the $180,000 development cost as an intangible non-current asset in its statement of financial position at 30 April 20X6. Amortisation will start from 1 May 20X6 when the new process starts operation.

238 The answer is **B and D.**

Item 1 relates to IAS 2 that states inventory should be valued at the lower of cost or NRV. The inventory has been overvalued by $500 and should be adjusted, however it is not material (only 3% of revenue) so it would be acceptable to adjust in the next set of financial statements.

Item 2 relates to IAS 38 that states development costs can only be capitalised if they meet the criteria of the standard. If the project has now been abandoned it does not meet the criteria and should be written off from the statement of financial position against profit. The CA of $600,000 is material and should be done immediately.

239 The answer is **B, D and E.**

Goodwill – purchased goodwill is the price paid over the value of the net assets of the business. In this scenario JX has paid $700,000 for a business worth $650,000, hence creating $50,000 of goodwill.

This will be shown in JX's statement of financial position as an intangible asset at 31 October 20X9 and will be subject to an impairment review by IFRS 3 Business Combinations each year.

240 The answer is **A, B and D.**

The development expenditure appears to meet the criteria of IAS 38 to defer expenditure, i.e. expect to complete, able to use or sell, profitable, etc.

Therefore, this will be shown in JX's statement of financial position at 31 October 20X9 at $590,000 ($90,000 purchased and $500,000 spent to complete) and it will be amortised over five years, beginning on 1 November 20X9.

241 The answer is **A and C.**

Brand Z was acquired as part of JX's business. IAS 38 sets out the conditions under which an intangible asset (such as a brand) can be recognised:

- it must be probable that future economic benefits will flow to the business, and

- the cost of the asset can be measured reliably.

In the situation in the question, both conditions apply. Presumably the valuation of $200,000 on purchase is a reliable measurement of the fair value of the brand at this date, so Brand Z can be recognised as a purchased intangible non-current asset in JX's statement of financial position.

In JX's statement of financial position at 31 October 20X9, the brand will be shown as:

	Cost	Accumulated amortisation	Carrying amount
Non-current assets	$000	$000	$000
Purchased brand	200	–	200

The brand cannot be shown at its revalued amount of $250,000 unless an active market exists, which we have no evidence of. The brand will be amortised over its useful life.

242 B

The earthquake occurred after the end of the accounting period. Assets and liabilities at 31 August 20X9 were not affected. The earthquake is indicative of conditions that arose after the reporting period and does not give any further evidence in relation to assets and liabilities in existence at the reporting date. Therefore according to IAS 10 Events after the Reporting Period it will be classified as a non-adjusting event after the reporting period. The cost of the repairs will be charged to the Statement of profit or loss and other comprehensive income in the period when it is incurred. Due to the impact on MN, i.e. closure and loss of earnings for 6 months, the earthquake and an estimate of its effect will need to be disclosed by way of a note in MN's financial statements for the year ended 31 August 20X9.

243

Treatment of the discontinued operation
The assets have met the criteria of an asset held for sale
The assets should be shown separately as assets held for sale in the statement of financial position
The assets should be valued at $398,000
Impairment of $45,000 should be treated as an expense to the statement of profit or loss

EK can treat the sale of its retailing division as a discontinued operation as defined by IFRS 5 Non-current Assets Held for Sale and Discontinued Operations as it is held for sale. There is a plan to dispose of the separate major line of business as a single transaction, such that the economic value of the assets will be realised by selling, rather than continuing to use them.

The assets should be recognised at the lower of:

- the value under normal accounting standards, i.e. $443,000

- the value on sale, being the fair value less the costs of sale, i.e. $423,000 less $25,000.

Therefore, EK should value the assets at $398,000.

This results in an impairment loss of $45,000 ($443,000 − $398,000), which should be recognised as an expense to the statement of profit or loss.

Once this valuation exercise has been performed, no depreciation or amortisation should be recognised.

The trading performance of the continuing divisions should be shown in the statement of profit or loss (or disclosed by way of note), as well as the overall performance, so that readers can evaluate the likely impact of the disposal.

244 The answer is **$170.**

Non-current assets – PPE

	$million		$million
Bfwd	645	Depn	120
		Disposal (CA)	60
Additions	170	Dep'n (balance)	635
	——		——
	815	Cfwd	815
	——		——

245 The answer is **$7.**

Non-current assets – investments

	$million		$million
Bfwd	107	Revaluation loss	21
Additions	7	Cfwd	93
	——		——
	114		114
	——		——

246 The answer is **$13.**

Non-current assets – developments

	$million		$million
Bfwd	24	Amortisation	8
Additions	13	Cfwd	29
	——		——
	37		37
	——		——

247

Item (i)	Item (ii)	Item (iii)
Treat as an intangible asset	Criteria of IAS 38 not met to capitalise	Criteria of IAS 38 not met to capitalise
Do not amortise in current year	Expense to the statement of profit or loss	Expense to the statement of profit or loss

This question required students to whether the expenditure gives rise to an asset under IAS 38. For an asset to be recognised as an intangible asset there must be a probable flow of benefit to the enterprise and you must be able to make a reliable estimate of cost.

- Item (i) can be recognised as an intangible asset if the author expects the book to be successful and profitable and it is probable. The cost would not be amortised until the book is actually published.

- Item (ii) did not have any additional sales and therefore there was no probable flow of a benefit to the enterprise. They also stated that no reliable estimate could be made, therefore the expense must be written off direct to the statement of profit or loss.

- Item (iii) is very difficult to measure whether there will be a probable benefit as a result of the advertising to improve the corporate image. It would also be hard to make a reliable estimate of cost and therefore should also be written off to the statement of profit or loss as an expense.

248 The answer is **B, C and D.**

As the error is material in terms of the profit previously reported for the prior year, a prior year adjustment should be made in accordance with IAS 8 Accounting Policies, Changes in Accounting Estimates and Errors. This will reduce the prior year profit and retained reserves brought forward by $45,000. The comparative figures in the financial statements would also be restated and the $45,000 would be excluded from the current year's figures. The nature of the error and the amount of the correction must be disclosed in the notes.

249 The answer is **$20,000 impairment.**

Building A	$
1.9.W6 Cost	200,000
Useful economic life	20
At first revaluation – 31.8.X1 – CA	200,000 × 15/20 =150,000
Revaluation gain/(loss)	30,000
Valuation carried forward	180,000
At second revaluation – 31.8.X6 – CA	180,000 × 10/15 = 120,000
Revaluation gain/(loss)	(20,000)
Revaluation	100,000

The impairment on A is less than the revaluation reserve of $30,000, so the impairment is debited against the revaluation reserve, leaving a balance on that reserve of $10,000.

250 DV should **reduce the revaluation reserve** for the **impairment** on Building A for the year ended 31 August 20X6.

251 The answer is **$7,500 impairment.**

Building B	$
1.9.W6 Cost	120,000
Useful economic life	15
At first revaluation – 31.8.X1 – CV	120,000 × 10/15 = 80,000
Revaluation gain/(loss)	(5,000)
Valuation carried forward	75,000
At second revaluation – 31.8.X6 – CV	75,000 × 5/10 = 37,500
Revaluation gain/(loss)	(7,500)
Revaluation	30,000

The impairment on B of $7,500 goes to the statement of profit or loss, as there is no revaluation reserve in respect of that building.

252 DV should **expense to the profit or loss** for the **impairment** on Building B for the year ended 31 August 20X6.

253 The answer is **$72,000.**

Proceeds from share issue = (460 + 82 – 400 – 70)

254 C

The inflow and outflow of the loans should be shown separately on the statement of cash flows.

Long term borrowings			
	$000		$000
Payments	25	B/fwd	105
C/fwd	129	**Additions**	49
	———		———
	154		154
	———		———

255 A

The carrying amount of Hotel K at 30 September is $430,000, which is $110,000 higher than its current valuation of $320,000. In compliance with the new accounting policy, Hotel K should be revalued to $320,000. The reduction in the statement of financial position valuation of $110,000 represents an impairment loss. This loss should be recognised as a charge in the statement of profit or loss for the year to 30 September 20X4.

256 B

Hotel G should be revalued to $650,000 and Hotel H to $820,000 from 1 January 20X4. The transfer to the revaluation reserve for Hotels G and H should be the difference between their carrying amount at 1 January 20X4 (before the revaluation) and their revalued amount. The carrying amount of the hotels is their cost less accumulated depreciation to 1 January 20X4. For Hotel G this was $346,000 ($650,000 – $304,000) and for Hotel H this was $126,000 ($820,000 – $694,000). This is a total of $472,000.

The reduction in value of Hotel K of $110,000 is not charged against this reserve.

257 A discontinued operation is a component of an entity that either has been disposed of or is classified as held for sale, and that represents a separate major line of **business** or **geographical area** of operations that is part of a single co-ordinated plan to dispose of a separate major line of **business** or **geographical area** of operations.

258

GK's statement of cash flow YE 31 October 20X8	$000
Profit before tax	2,200
Finance cost	600
Depreciation	1,992
Gain on disposal of assets	(25)
Inventory	(250)
Receivables	(150)
Payables	(70)
	–––––
Cash generated from operations	4,297
	–––––

259 D

Tax liability

	$000		$000
Bank	750	Bfwd	1,200
Cfwd	1,449	Profit or loss	999
	–––––		–––––
	2,199		2,199
	–––––		–––––

260 B

Interest liability

	$000		$000
Bank	870	Bfwd	600
Cfwd	330	Profit or loss	600
	–––––		–––––
	1,200		1,200
	–––––		–––––

261   The answer is **$1,977,000.**

<table>
<tr><th colspan="4" align="center">Non-current assets</th></tr>
<tr><td></td><td>$000</td><td></td><td>$000</td></tr>
<tr><td>Bfwd</td><td>10,500</td><td>Depn (1,110 + 882)</td><td>1,992</td></tr>
<tr><td>Bfwd</td><td>4,550</td><td>Disposal (CA)</td><td>35</td></tr>
<tr><td>Additions</td><td>1,977</td><td>Cfwd</td><td>10,000</td></tr>
<tr><td></td><td></td><td>Cfwd</td><td>5,000</td></tr>
<tr><td></td><td>17,027</td><td></td><td>17,027</td></tr>
</table>

262   The answer is **$600,000.**

Cash flows from financing activities	$000
Dividends paid	(500)
Issue of share capital (2,500 + 6,000 – 1,000 – 3,000)	4,500
Redemption of interest bearing borrowings	(4,600)
	(600)

263   The answer is **A, C and D.**

264   C

The brand must be valued at the lower of carrying amount ($250,000) and recoverable amount ($230,000), i.e. $230,000. Recoverable amount is the higher of (a) fair value less costs to sell ($230,000) and (b) value in use ($150,000).

Working:

	$
Cost	500,000
Accumulated amortisation (500,000 × 5/10)	(250,000)
Carrying amount	250,000

The impairment loss of $20,000 ($250,000 – $230,000) must be charged to the statement of profit or loss in the year ended 30 September 20X5.

265 **B**

Building

	$
Cost	1,000,000
Y/e 30/9/X3 – Depreciation (1,000,000/20)	(50,000)
Y/e 30/9/X4 – Depreciation (1,000,000/20)	(50,000)
Carrying amount	900,000
Revaluation	1,800,000
Credit to revaluation reserve	900,000

266 The answer is **$100,000.**

Depreciation will be based on the revalued figure: $1,800,000/18 years.

267 **C**

Following the revaluation, depreciation must be calculated on the revalued figure. There seems to have been no change to the estimate of the building's life, so 18 years of life remain.

Y/e 30/9/X5	$
Valuation b/f	1,800,000
Depreciation (1,800,000/18)	(100,000)
Carrying amount	1,700,000
Revaluation	1,500,000
Debit to revaluation reserve	200,000

As the building had previously been revalued, the impairment loss can be debited to the revaluation reserve rather than being charged to the statement of profit or loss.

268 The answer is **$88,235.**

Future depreciation will be based on the revalued figure: $1,500,000/17 years = $88,235 p.a.

269 **C**

270 **B**

271 The answer is **D and E.**

272

	Statement of profit or loss		Statement of financial position
	$		$
Depreciation	40,000	Non-current asset	160,000
Grant income	6,000	Government grant current liability	6,000
		Government grant non-current liability	18,000

Non-current asset = $200,000 – depreciation at 20% $40,000 = $160,000

The grant is credited to the liability account and then released to the statement of profit or loss over the assets life, i.e. 20% × $30,000 = $6,000 pa

273

	Statement of profit or loss		Statement of financial position
	$		$
Depreciation	34,000	Non-current asset	136,000
Grant income	0	Government grant current liability	0
		Government grant non-current liability	0

Non-current asset = $200,000 – $30,000 = $170,000 depreciation at 20% $34,000 = $136,000

The grant is credited to the asset account and will therefore reduce the amount to be depreciated each year.

274

		$
Debit	Statement of profit or loss	6,000
Debit	Deferred income	15,000
Credit	Bank	21,000

275 IAS 40 Investment Property defines an investment property as **land or a buildings held to earn rentals, or for capital appreciation or both, rather than for use in the entity or for sale by the entity in the ordinary course of business.**

276 D

The sale is recorded at the exchange rate of £400,000/.65 = $615,385

277 A

The payment is recorded at the exchange rate of £400,000/.6 = $666,667

This amount is debited to the bank.

The receivables will be credited with $615,385 and therefore the difference will be credited to the statement of profit or loss as a gain.

278 IAS 21 The Effects of Changes in Foreign Exchange Rates states unsettled **monetary** items at the reporting date must be **retranslated using the closing rate** and unsettled **non-monetary** items are **left at historical rate.**

279 A

The sale is recorded at the exchange rate of 200,000/1.65 = $121,212

280 C

The sale is retranslated at the exchange rate of 200,000/1.86 = $107,527

This will reduce receivables by $13,685 and debit the statement of profit or loss as a loss. No adjustment should be made to the sales account.

281 B

The payment is recorded at the exchange rate of 200,000/1.91 = $104,712

This amount is debited to the bank.

The receivables will be credited with $107,527 and therefore the difference will be debited to the statement of profit or loss as a loss.

282

	Defined contribution	**Defined benefit**
Characteristic	The employer's contribution is usually a fixed percentage of the employee's salary	The employer undertakes to finance a pension income of a certain amount, e.g. 2/3 × final salary × (years of service/40 years)
Characteristic	The employer has no further obligation after this amount is paid	The employer has an ongoing obligation to make sufficient contributions to the plan to fund the pensions
Characteristic	The annual cost to the employer is reasonably predictable	The cost of providing pensions is not certain and varies from year to year

283 The answer is **$105,000.**

$3.5 million × 3% = $105,000

284 The answer is **$9,000.**

Payments have been made during the year of $8,000 × 12 = $96,000

An accrual of $9,000 is required.

285 When an entity has a defined benefit pension scheme it recognises the net defined benefit liability (or asset) in the statement of financial position. If the plan has a liability it is measured at the **present value** of the defined benefit obligation and if the plan has an asset it is measured at the **fair value** at the reporting date.

286

Statement of profit or loss (debit)	Statement of profit or loss (credit)	Statement of financial position (debit asset)	Statement of financial position (credit liability)
Current and past service costs	Interest income (on asset)	Interest income (on asset)	Current and past service costs
Interest cost (on liability)			Interest cost (on liability)

287 The answer is a **gain** of **$4 million.**

	$ million
Net liability b/fwd	(40)
Net interest cost (40 × 10%)	(4)
Current service cost	(35)
Past service costs	(12)
Pension contributions paid	35
Gain (balance)	**4**
Net liability c/fwd	(52)

288 The answer **is $51 million.**

Current service cost $35 + past service cost $12 + interest $4 = $51 million.

The gain of $4 million has no effect on profit as treated as other comprehensive income in the statement of profit or loss.

289 **A**

	$
Cost of investment	1,400,000
Reserves at acquisition – (600,000 × 0.50) + $50,000	(350,000)
	1,050,000
Impairment 60%	(630,000)
Goodwill at 31 December 20X8	420,000

290 C

	$
Cost of investment	100,000
Reserves at acquisition –	
$30,000 + $50,000	(80,000)
NCI (20% × $80,000)	16,000
	36,000
Impairment 60%	(21,600)
Goodwill at 31 December 20X9	14,400

	$
Reserves of Tom	400,000
Post-acquisition reserves of Jerry –	
($50,000 + $50,000) – ($50,000 + $30,000) × 80%	16,000
Impairment (above working)	(21,600)
Total reserves at 31 December 20X9	394,400

291 D

	$
Cost of investment	750,000
Reserves at acquisition –	
$20,000 + $10,000	(30,000)
NCI (40% × $30,000)	12,000
	732,000
Impairment 20%	(146,400)
Goodwill at 31 December 20X9	585,600

292 A

	$
Cost of investment	35,000
Reserves at acquisition –	
$20,000 + $10,000	(30,000)
NCI at fair value	4,000
	9,000
Impairment 20%	(1,800)
Goodwill at 31 December 20X9	7,200

	$
Reserves of Gary	40,000
Post-acquisition reserves of Barlow –	
($20,000 + $15,000) – ($20,000 + $10,000) × 90%	4,500
Impairment (above working $1,800 × 90%)	(1,620)
Total reserves at 31 December 20X9	42,880

293 The answer is **$84,000.**

Cost of investment	300,000
Reserves at acquisition –	
$200,000 + $60,000	(260,000)
NCI ($260,000 × 25%)	65,000
	105,000
Impairment 20%	(21,000)
Goodwill at 31 December 20X9	84,000

294 The answer is **$28,600.**

Net assets of SB

	Date of acquisition
	$
$1 equity shares	150,000
Share premium	15,000
Retained earnings	(22,000)
	143,000

Goodwill

	$
Cost of investment	185,000
Net assets of SB at acquisition (as above)	(143,000)
NCI ($143,000 × 20%)	28,600
Goodwill at acquisition	70,600

295 The answer is **$25,900.**

Investment in associate

	$
Cost of investment	25,000
Profits after dividends (6,500 − 3,500) × 30%	900
Investment in associate	25,900

296 A

Total PUP = $33,000/125 × 25 = $6,600 × 50% still in inventory = $3,300

297 A

	$
Reserves of Stress	1,500,000
Post-acquisition reserves of Full −	
($1,600,000 + $500,000) − ($1,600,000 + $300,000) × 80%	160,000
Total reserves at 30 September 20X9	1,660,000

298 D

NCI = $1,600,000 + $500,000 × 20% = $420,000

299 The answer is **B and D.**

	$	
Sales value	168	150%
Cost value	112	100%
Profit	56	50%

Workings:

Mark up means profit is based on cost, therefore cost represents 100%. If profit is 50%, the sales value must be worth 150%. $36,000 of goods are still in stock. This represents 150%.

The profit element = $36,000/150 × 50 = $12,000

The closing inventory will be reduced by the PUP which results in an increase in cost of sales.

300 The answer is **$1,000,000.**

	$m	
Sales value	24	100%
Cost value	18	75%
Profit	6	25%

Workings:

Profit is $6m and represents 25% of the selling price.

$4m of goods are still in stock (24–20). The profit element = $4m × 25% = $1m

301 A

NCI = sub (PAT $6,000,000 – $1,000,000 (PUP) – $600,000 (impairment)) × 25% = $1,100,000

The subsidiary is the seller so PUP will reduce the subs profits

Impairment is charged against the subsidiary profit if the FV method of valuing NCI is used

302 D

Revenue = 120 + 48 – 24 (inter-company) = $144m

Cost of sales = 84 + 40 – 24 + 1 (PUP) = $101m

303 C

		$000
Revenue (above Qu 281)		144,000
Cost of sales (above Qu 281)		(101,000)
Gross profit		43,000
Distribution cost	5,000 + 100	(5,100)
Administration expense	7,000 + 300 + 600	(7,900)
Profit from operations		30,000
Investment income		150
Finance cost		(400)
Tax	6,000 + 1,200	(7,200)
Profit for the year		22,550
Attributable to:		
Parent (balance)		21,450
NCI (above Qu 280)		1,100
		22,550

304 A

Non-current assets = 1,918,000 + 1,960,000 = 3,878,000

Note: We do not include the associates assets and liabilities in the consolidated statement of financial position.

305 The answer is **$627,200.**

Cost of investment	448,000
Post-acquisition reserves –	
($896,000 – $280,000) × 30%	184,800
Impairment	(5,600)
Investment in associate	627,200

306 The goodwill amount to be shown in the consolidated statement of financial position is **$198,800.**

Cost of investment	1,610,000
Reserves at acquisition –	
$1,680,000 – $112,000	(1,568,000)
NCI ($1,680,000 – $112,000) × 10%	156,800
	198,800

Note: The subsidiary has losses at the date of acquisition, hence are deducted from the ordinary share capital.

307 B

		$
Non-current assets		
Property, plant and equipment	1,918 + 1,960	3,878,000
Goodwill	(above Qu 285)	198,800
Investment in associate	(above Qu 284)	627,200
		4,704,000
Current assets		
Inventory	760 + 1,280	2,040,000
Receivables	380 + 620	1,000,000
Cash	70 + 116	186,000
		7,930,000

308 **A**

Retained earnings of Really	2,464,000
Post-acquisition RE –	
($1,204,000 + $112,000) × 90%	1,184,400
($896,000 – $280,000) × 30%	184,800
Impairment	(5,600)
	3,827,600

309 The NCI amount to be shown in the consolidated statement of financial position is **$288,400.** NCI should be shown as **equity.**

NCI = $2,884,000 × 10% = $288,400

310 The answer is **$185,000.**

Net assets of DN	Date of acquisition
	$000
$1 equity shares	180
Share premium	40
Retained earnings	60
	280

Goodwill	
	$000
Cost of investment (90% × 180 × $2.50)	405
+ FV of NCI at acquisition	60
– Net Assets at acquisition (180 + 60 + 40)	(280)
Goodwill at acquisition	185

311

Purchased goodwill	Internally generated goodwill
Treat as an intangible asset	Not recognised in the financial statements
Undertake an impairment review each year	Not capable of a reliable measurement

312 The acquisition of 80,000 preferred shares will **not give control or any influence** because the preferred shares **have no voting rights.** Therefore this investment would be classified as **a non-current investment** in HI's financial statements.

313 The acquisition of 40,000 equity shares and 30,000 preferred shares will give HI a **40%** interest in ABC, this would be sufficient to give **significant influence** of ABC. ABC would be classified as **an associate.**

314 The acquisition of **70,000 equity shares** will give HI a 70% interest in ABC, this would be sufficient to give **control** of ABC. ABC would be classified as **a subsidiary.**

315 C

If an impairment review indicates that goodwill has increased in value, the increase is deemed to be internally generated goodwill. IAS 38 Intangible Assets does not allow internally generated goodwill to be recognised in financial statements.

JK will therefore not recognise the increase in goodwill and will include goodwill in its statement of financial position at its original value of $100,000.

Goodwill in B was impaired, so according to IFRS 3 Business Combinations goodwill in the consolidated financial statements must be reduced. $20,000 will be charged to JK's statement of profit or loss for the year ended 31 March 20X4 and must be deducted from the goodwill balance in JK's statement of financial position at 31 March 20X4.

The total goodwill figure shown in JK's statement of financial position at 31 March 20X4 will be $190,000.

	$000	$000
	A	*B*
Cost of acquisition	850	610
Fair value of net assets at date of acquisition	(750)	(500)
Goodwill at acquisition	100	110
Impairment	–	(20)
Goodwill at 31 March 20X4	100	90

316 A subsidiary entity is an entity, including an unincorporated entity such as a partnership, which is controlled by another entity (known as the parent).

Control is the power to govern the financial and operating policies of an entity so as to obtain benefit from its activities. A controlling interest is usually obtained by acquiring more than **50% of the equity shares.**

An associated entity is an entity where another entity can exercise significant influence over the financial and operating policy decisions of that entity. Significant influence is not control over those policies. Significant influence is normally assumed to exist if an entity acquires **20% or more of another entity's equity share capital.**

317

Investment in CD	Investment in EF
Treat as an associate	Treat as a subsidiary
Has significant influence	Has effective control
Exercises control of 40%	Exercises control of 40%

According to IFRS 10 Consolidated financial statements a subsidiary is an entity that is controlled by another entity.

IFRS 10 defines control as the power to govern the financial and operating policies of an entity so as to obtain benefit from its activities.

There is a presumption that control exists where an investor entity owns 50% or more of the voting rights of the entity. A parent/subsidiary relationship can also be created when the parent entity owns less than 50% of voting rights but is able to exercise control through another means.

CD is not a subsidiary of AB.

AB has acquired 40% of the voting rights and 80% of the non-voting shares. Overall AB is only able to exercise control over 40% of CD's voting rights so cannot exercise control.

EF is a subsidiary of AB.

AB has acquired 40% of the voting rights of EF. AB also has the power to remove and appoint all of EF's directors.

AB can therefore control the management of EF and can exercise control of EF. As a result EF is a subsidiary of AB.

318 A

319 D

320 B

Mark-up on cost 33 1/3% =

Goods left in inventory $6,000/133.33333 × 33.3333% = $1,500

321 B

MANAGEMENT OF WORKING CAPITAL, CASH AND SOURCES OF SHORT-TERM FINANCE

322 C

Businesses that regularly fail to pay their suppliers on time may find it difficult to obtain future credit.

323 D

A conservative working capital policy is one which only uses short-term financing for part of the fluctuating current assets.

324 The answer is **$755,760.**

		Cash received
		$
April sales	20% × $780,000	156,000
March sales	80% × 0.98 × $770,000 × 60%	362,208
February sales	80% × 0.98 × $760,000 × 30%	178,752
January sales	80% × 0.98 × $750,000 × 10%	58,800
		—————
		755,760
		—————

325 **B**

The current ratio is all current assets including inventory divided by current liabilities, while the acid test is the current asset figure less inventory divided by current liabilities. These can only be equal if an entity carries no inventory.

326 The answer is **$4,800.**

	Current assets	Current liabilities
	$	$
Credit purchase:		
Inventory	+ 18,000	
Trade payables		+ 18,000
Credit sale:		
Trade receivables	+ 24,000	
Inventory (24,000 × 100/125)	− 19,200	

Working capital will increase by $4,800, as a result of the credit sale.

327 The answer is **$252,000.**

	$
Budgeted sales	240,000
Expected decrease in receivables	12,000
	—————
	252,000
	—————

The reduction in receivables means that the entity will expect to receive more cash next month than the total of its credit sales for the month. Changes in inventory levels have no effect on expected cash receipts.

328 The answer is **47 days.**

Receivables

	$		$
B/f	68,000	Returns	2,500
Sales	250,000	Cash	252,100
		Irrecoverable debts	
		(68,000 × 0.05)	3,400
		C/f	60,000
	_____		_____
	318,000		318,000
	_____		_____

Receivable days = 64/495 × 365 = 47.19 days, round down to 47 days

Average receivables = 68 + 60/2 = $64,000

(Note: That the estimated sales cover a period of only six months, so the annual sales figure is $495,000 (2 × 250,000 – 2,500.)

329 B

Working capital cycle		*Days*
Inventory	(8/30) × 365	97.3
Trade receivables	(4/40) × 365	36.5
Trade payables	(3/15) × 365	(73.0)
		_____
Cash conversion cycle		60.8
		_____

Note: The annual cost of purchases would be useful for measuring the inventory turnover period for raw materials. Since the question does not state whether inventory is mainly raw materials, work-in-progress or finished goods, it is probably appropriate to use the annual cost of sales to measure the average inventory turnover time. However, it is probably reasonable to assume that most trade payables relate to purchases of raw materials, and the annual purchases figure has therefore been used to calculate the payment cycle for trade payables.

330 C

Average receivables = ($10 million + $12 million)/2 = $11 million

Average trade-related receivables = 90% × $11 million = $9.9 million

Annual sales on credit = $95 million

Average collection period = (9.9 million/95 million) × 365 days = 38 days

331 B

	$
Balance b/fwd	22,000
Credit sales	290,510
	312,510
Less: Balance c/fwd ($290,510 × 49/365)	(39,000)
Receipts	273,510

332 The answer is **$345,000.**

	$
Purchases on credit	360,000
Increase in trade payables	(15,000)
Therefore payments to suppliers	345,000

333 C

($82,000 – 12,250) × 97% = $67,657

334 The answer is **$345,589.**

	$
Owed to credit suppliers at 1 November 20X6	42,000
Cost of goods sold	350,000
Less: Opening inventory reflected in cost of goods sold	(56,000)
Add: Closing inventory deducted from cost of goods sold	
60/365 × 350,000	57,534
Less: Amounts owed to credit suppliers at 31 October 20X7	
50/365 × 350,000	(47,945)
Amount paid to credit suppliers during the year to 31 October 20X7	345,589

335 The answer is **88 days.**

Trade receivable days = 290/2,400 × 365 = 44.1 days

Inventory days (assuming that inventories are finished goods) = 360/1,400 × 365 = 93.9 days

Trade payable days = 190/1,400 × 365 = 49.6 days

Working capital cycle = Inventory days + Receivable days – Payable days

= 93.9 + 44.1 – 49.6 = 88.4 days, round down to 88 days

336 The answer is **$19,800.**

Sales in	Total sales	Cash sales	Credit sales		Received in May
	$	$	$		$
April	20,000	8,000	12,000	(97% × 12,000)	11,640
May	20,400	8,160	12,240		8,160
					_____
					19,800
					_____

337 B

Overtrading is associated with fast-growing companies that have insufficient long-term capital, and rely on short-term liabilities to finance their growth. The finance is largely provided by suppliers (trade payables) and a bank overdraft. As a result, there is an increasing bank overdraft (higher borrowing) and very low or even negative working capital. A typical overtrading enterprise is experiencing rapid growth and rising sales. Although it should be profitable, its problem will be a shortage of cash and liquidity. Cash balances will be not be rising, since the overdraft is increasing.

338 An aged trade creditor's analysis (aged trade payables analysis) **is a breakdown of trade payables according to length of time elapsing since the purchase was made.**

An aged analysis for trade payables is an analysis of unpaid invoices from suppliers according to the length of time since the issue of the invoice. It is not a list (therefore answer A and answer B are incorrect), but a table. A spreadsheet might be used to construct the analysis. The analysis can be used to decide which suppliers should be paid, and how much.

An aged analysis for trade receivables is similar, except that it relates to unpaid invoices sent to credit customers. This analysis is used to decide which customers to 'chase' for payment.

339 B

Under the Miller-Orr model, the greater the variability in cash flows, the greater is the spread between the upper and lower cash balance limits. The return point is the lower limit plus one-third of the spread.

340 The answer is **$42,000.**

Using the Miller-Orr model, the size of the spread between the lower limit and upper limit should be:

$$\text{Spread} = 3 \left[\frac{^3/_4 \times \text{Transaction cost} \times \text{Variance of cash flow}}{\text{Interest rate}} \right]^{1/3}$$

$$= 3 \left[\frac{^3/_4 \times 40 \times 4,000^2}{0.0004} \right]^{1/3}$$

= $31,879. To the nearest $, this is $32,000.

Upper limit = Lower limit + Spread= $10,000 + $32,000 = $42,000

341 The answer is **$9,000.**

$$\text{Spread} = 3\left[\frac{^3/_4 \times 30 \times 300,000}{0.00025}\right]^{1/_3} = 9,000$$

342 The answer is **$5,500.**

Return point = 2,500 + (9,000 × 1/3) = 5,500

343 The answer is **$11,500.**

Upper limit = 2,500 + 9,000 = 11,500

344 The answer is **$17,000.**

$$\text{Optimal amount} = \sqrt{\frac{2\times30\times(12\times20,000)}{0.05}}$$

= $16,970

To the nearest $100, this is $17,000.

345 **C**

The equivalent annual return offered by supplier P is:

$(100/99)^{12} - 1 = 12.82\%$

This is below the minimum required rate of return of 12.85% and should not be accepted.

The equivalent annual return offered by supplier Q is:

$(100/98)^{12/2} - 1 = 12.89\%$

This is just above the minimum required rate of return of 12.85% and therefore should be accepted.

346 The answer is **27.86%.**

Annual rate of interest = $(100/98)^{(365/30 - 0)} - 1$

= 0.2786 or 27.86%

347 The answer is **A, C and E.**

348 Invoice discounting normally involves **selling an individual invoice for cash to a factor organisation at a discount.**

Invoice discounting is a method of obtaining short-term funds. Specific invoices are 'sold' to a finance organisation, typically a factor, which provides finance up to a proportion (about 70%) of the value of the invoice. The invoice discounter is repaid with interest out of the money from the invoice payment, when it is eventually paid.

349 D

If $1 million is invested for one year at 7%, the value of the investment will be $1,000,000 × 1.07 = $1,070,000 after one year.

If $1 million is invested for three months at 6.5% per year and then for nine months at 7.5% per year, this means that the interest for the first three months will be 6.5% × 3/12 = 1.625%, and the interest for the next nine months will be 7.5% × 9/12 = 5.625%. The value of the investment after one year will therefore be:

$1,000,000 × 1.01625 × 1.05625 = $1,073,414.

This is $3,414 more than the income that would be obtained by investing at 7% for the full year. However, there is a risk that interest rates will not rise during the first three months, and XYZ will not be able to invest at 7.5% for the nine months, but only at a lower rate.

350 A

The customer cannot be asked for immediate payment once a bill of exchange has been accepted.

351 C

The instrument is a bill of exchange drawn on the bank. This is often called a bank bill (as distinct from a commercial bill, which is a bill drawn on a non-bank company). A bill drawn on a bank under a short-term financing arrangement is also known as an acceptance credit.

352 A

Forfaiting is a method of obtaining medium-term export finance, involving the issue of promissory notes by the importer/buyer, which the exporter is able to sell to a forfaiting bank at a discount to obtain finance. Promissory notes are promises to pay a specified amount of money at a specified future date. The importer's promissory notes have settlement dates spread over a number of years, often the expected useful economic life of the imported items. The importer is therefore able to pay for the imported goods over a period of several years, whilst the exporter can obtain immediate payment by selling the promissory notes.

353

Forms of short-term finance
Trade payables
Factoring
Invoice discounting

The other items are forms of short-term investments.

354 The answer is **41.2%.**

AL offers 1.5% interest for 16 days

(100/98.5) (365/16) – 1 =

(1.015) 22.8125 – 1 = 41.2%

355 A

Working capital financing involves deciding the mix of long-term and short-term debt. An aggressive policy involves using short-term finance to fund all the fluctuating current assets, as well as some of the permanent part of the current assets. So answer A is correct. A conservative policy is where all of the permanent assets (i.e. non-current assets and the permanent part of current assets) are financed by long-term funding. Short-term financing is only used for part of the fluctuating current assets. So answer B is incorrect. A moderate policy matches short-term finance to the fluctuating current assets and long-term finance to the permanent part of current assets plus non-current assets. So answer D is also incorrect.

356 The answer is **14.8%**.

Annual cost = $(100/98.5)^{(365/(60-20))} - 1$

= $(100/98.5)^{9.125} - 1$

= 14.8%

357

		Aged analysis	
		$	
June		295	
July		0	
August		231	
September		319	
		——	
		845	
		——	

Workings:

	$
June debts: 345 + 520 + 150 − 200 − 520	295
July debts: 233 − 233	0
Augusts debts: 197 + 231 − 197	231
September debts: 319	319
	——
	845
	——

358 B

(70,000 + 10,000) : (88,000 + 7,000)

80,000 : 95,000

0.84 : 1

359 The answer is **500 units.**

Optimal order quantity = $\sqrt{\dfrac{2\times200\times10,000}{[4+(3\%\times400)]}}$

= 500 units

360 B

With JIT purchasing, the objective is to receive deliveries exactly at the time required, so that the ideal inventory level is always 0. Therefore inventory holding costs should be lower. There will be an increased dependence on suppliers to deliver exactly on time, but there will be a risk (probably an increased risk) of inventory shortages due to failure by suppliers to deliver on time. However, since purchases will be made to meet demand requirements, there are likely to be much more frequent deliveries.

361 A

The simple EOQ model formula is:

$EOQ = \sqrt{\dfrac{2cd}{h}}$

Where: d = annual demand

h = cost of holding one unit for one year

c = cost of placing order

362 C

$EOQ = \sqrt{\dfrac{2C_oD}{C_h}} = \sqrt{\dfrac{2\times\$185\times2,500}{\$25}}$

$= \sqrt{37,000}$

= 192 units

Each week $\dfrac{2,500}{52}$ = 48 units are required.

Therefore each order of 192 units will last $\dfrac{192}{48}$ = 4 weeks.

363 The answer is **895 units.**

$\sqrt{\dfrac{2\times\$15\times32,000}{\$1.2}} = \sqrt{800,000} = 894.43\,\text{units} = \text{rounded to 895 units}$

364 The answer is **A, B and C.**

The cost of placing an order under the EOQ formula includes administrative costs, postage and quality control costs.

365 The answer is **98 orders.**

$$Q = \sqrt{\frac{2C_oD}{C_h}}$$

$$\sqrt{\frac{2 \times 15 \times 95,000}{3}} = 974.68$$

95,000/975 = 97.4.

366 The answer is **10.5%.**

The yield to maturity must be more than the coupon rate of 7% as the purchase price of the bond is less than maturity value. Using the maths tables to compute the present values of the sums receivable under the bond, the maturity value can be calculated as follows:

t = 8; r = 10

(7 × 5.335) + (100 × 0.467) = 37.345 + 46.7 = $84.045

t = 8; r = 11

(7 × 5.146) + (100 × 0.434) = 36.022 + 43.4 + $79.422

By interpolation:

10% + ((84.045 − 82.0)/(84.045 − 79.422)) = 10% + (2.045/4.623) = 10.44%

367 The answer is **$8,864.**

$700 × (Annuity factor for t = 5; r = 10) + 10,000 × (Discount factor t = 5; r = 10) =

($700 × 3.791) + (10,000 × 0.621) = 2,653.7 + 6,210 = $8,863.70, rounded to $8,864

368 The answer is **7.2%**

Using t = 7 and r = 6 and 8, from tables

(4 × 5.582) and (100 × 0.665) = 22.328 + 66.5 = 88.828

(4 × 5.206) and (100 × 0.583) = 20.824 + 58.3 = 79.124

$$6 + \left\{ \frac{88.828 - 83.00}{88.828 - 79.124} \right\} \times 2 = 6 + \left\{ \frac{5.828}{9.704} \times 2 \right\}$$

6 + 1.20 = 7.20%

369 The answer is **7.77%.**

Interest = 0.06 × 100 = 6 pa for 10 years

Gain on redemption = 100 − 88 = 12

The yield to maturity is effectively the internal rate of return of the bond, which is found by trial and error. Let us assume a discount rate of 8% for the first calculation:

Time	Cash flow	Discount factor @ 8%	Discounted cash flow
	$		$
T_0	(88)	1	(88)
$T_1 - T_{10}$	6	6.710	40.26
T_{10}	100	0.463	46.3
			(1.44)

As this gives an NPV close to zero, use 7% for our next calculation:

Time	Cash flow	Discount factor @ 7%	Discounted cash flow
	$		$
T_0	(88)	1	(88)
$T_1 - T_{10}$	6	7.024	42.14
T_{10}	100	0.508	50.8
			4.94

Change in NPV between 7% and 8% is 6.38 (4.94 + 1.44) so, to get an NPV of zero, rate needs to be:

8% − 1.44/6.38 = 8 − 0.23 = 7.77%

370 The answer is **$869.**

$70 × (Annuity factor for t = 6; r = 10) + 1,000 × (Discount factor t = 6; r = 10) =

($70 × 4.355) + (1,000 × 0.564) = 304.85 + 564 = $868.85, rounded to $869

371

	May	June	July
	$000	$000	$000
Cash receipts	35	40	40
Credit sale receipts	101	104	111
	——	——	——
	136	144	151
	——	——	——

Workings:

Credit sales – receipts

	Total	May	June	July
	$000	$000	$000	$000
February	100	5		
March	100	30	5	
April	110	66	33	6
May	110		66	33
June	120			72
		——	——	——
Totals		101	104	111
		——	——	——

372

	May	June	July
	$000	$000	$000
Credit purchase payments	50	54	55

Credit purchases – payments

	Total	May	June	July
	$000	$000	$000	$000
March	50	15		
April	50	35	15	
May	55		39	16
June	55			39
		——	——	——
Totals		50	54	55
		——	——	——

373

Cash budget	May	June	July
	$000	$000	$000
Cash sales	35	40	40
Receipts from credit sales (Q371)	101	104	111
Total receipts	136	144	151
Payments for purchases (Q372)	50	54	55
Expenses paid	50	50	50
Equipment			250
Total payments	100	104	355
Net cash	36	40	(204)
Balance b/f	96	132	172
Balance c/f	132	172	(32)

374 The answer is **$16,961.**

Baumol

$$\text{Optimal sale} = \sqrt{\frac{2 \times \text{Annual cash disbursed} \times \text{Cost per sale}}{\text{Interest rate}}}$$

$$= \sqrt{\frac{2 \times 420,000 \times 25}{0.073}}$$

$$= 16,961$$

375 The answer **is $2,035.**

Miller-Orr

$$\text{Spread} = 3 \left[\frac{0.75 \times \text{Transaction cost} \times \text{Variance}}{\text{Interest rate}} \right]$$

$$= 3 \left[\frac{0.75 \times 25 \times 90,000}{0.0002} \right]^{1/3}$$

$$= 3 \sqrt[3]{8,437,500,000}$$

$$= 3 \times 2035.8$$

$$= 6,107$$

Under the Miller-Orr model, DJ should sell securities when the cash reaches the lower limit of $1,000. The amount sold should be sufficient to bring the cash back up to the return point, which is equal to the lower limit plus one-third of the spread(i.e. $1,000 + 1/3 × $6,107) = $3,305. As there is already a minimum cash holding of $1,000, this means that the optimum amount of securities to be sold is ($3,035 − $1000) = $2,035

376 The answer is **14.9%**.

Annual equivalent rate of interest

$$\left(\frac{100}{97}\right)^{\frac{365}{80}} -1 = 14.9\%$$

Note: An approximate rate of interest can be calculated as:

$$\frac{3}{(100-3)} \times \frac{365}{(90-10)} \times 100\% = 14.11\%$$

The more exact answer, however, is 14.9%, as shown.

377

Factors to consider for offering a discount
Borrowing on overdraft might be more risky
It is cheaper to finance the higher receivables by borrowing than it would be to offer the cash settlement discount
Other customers might demand the same settlement discount terms as FF
The cash settlement discount arrangement may be difficult to withdraw at a future time, if DF no longer wants to offer it

1   The bank would charge annual interest of 12% which is less than the rate above. This means that it is cheaper to finance the higher receivables by borrowing than it would be to offer the cash settlement discount.

2   If DF borrows on overdraft from a bank, there is a risk that the bank might withdraw or reduce the overdraft facility without notice. Borrowing on overdraft might therefore be more risky.

3   Other customers might demand the same settlement discount terms as FF.

4   Once it has been established, the cash settlement discount arrangement may be difficult to withdraw at a future time, if DF no longer wants to offer it.

378 The answer is **27.86 %**.

Taking the discount is equivalent to receiving interest at a rate of 27.86%. Therefore if DN needs to increase its overdraft to make the payment, it is beneficial to do so as long as the interest rate charged is less than 27.86%.

Alternatively, it would be beneficial for DN to use any surplus cash in its current account or cash in any short-term investments yielding less than 27.86%,.

Workings:

If DN pays $98 on day 10 instead of day 40, it will need to borrow $98 for 30 days.

The effective annual interest rate is:

$$\frac{365}{30} = 12.1667\%$$

$$1 + r = \left\{\frac{100}{98}\right\}^{12.1667}$$

$$1 + r = 1.2786$$

$$r = 0.2786 \text{ or } 27.86\%$$

379 The answer is **$152,000.**

Annual sales $2 million × 12 = £24 million.

			$
Factor's annual fee	(2.5% × $24 million)		(600,000)
Saving in administration costs			300,000

		$	
Current average receivables	($24 million × 90/360)	6,000,000	
Receivables with the factor	(0.20 × $24m × 60/360)	800,000	
		————	
Reduction in average receivables		5,200,000	

Savings in interest at 9%			468,000
Factor finance interest	((0.80 × $24m × 60/360 × 10%)		(320,000)
			————
Net annual cost			(152,000)

380 The answer is **$648.**

Cost of debt collection service

Reduction in average collection period for receivables = 20 days

Reduction in average trade receivables = 20/365 × $65,500 = $3,589

	$
Saving in interest cost of finance (9% × $3,589)	323
Reduction in irrecoverable debts (50% × $2,000)	1,000
	———
Total benefits	1,323
Fee payable for the service (1% × $67,500)	675
	———
Net annual benefit from using the service	648

381

	$	$	$
Extra contribution (35% × extra sales)	336,000	420,000	504,000
Advertising costs	(300,000)	(300,000)	(300,000)
Extra administration costs	(30,000)	(40,000)	(50,000)
Increase in irrecoverable debts	(35,400)	(39,000)	(42,600)
Extra cost of financing receivables (10% × extra receivables)	(28,000)	(33,333)	(38,667)
	———	———	———
Net effect on annual profit	(57,400)	7,667	72,733

Calculations of the net benefit or loss under each projected possible increase in sales are as follows:

	20%	25%	30%
	$	$	$
Original sales	4,800,000	4,800,000	4,800,000
Increase in annual sales	960,000	1,200,000	1,440,000
Total annual export sales	5,760,000	6,000,000	6,240,000
Irrecoverable debts:			
Current amount (note 1)	51,000	51,000	51,000
New irrecoverable debts (note 2)	86,400	90,000	93,600
Increase in irrecoverable debts	35,400	39,000	42,600
Current export trade receivables (note 3)	1,000,000	1,000,000	1,000,000
New amount of receivables (note 4)	1,280,000	1,333,333	1,386,667
Increase in export trade receivables	280,000	333,333	386,667
Annual cost at 10% interest	28,000	33,333	38,667

Notes:

1. Irrecoverable debts: Current

   Existing credit sales = $4.8m

   Less 15% = $4.08m

   Irrecoverable debts = 1.25% = $51,000

   Current = 1.25% × 85% × $4,800,000 = $51,000

2. Irrecoverable debts: Revised

   1.5% × $5,760,000 = $86,400

   1.5% × $6,000,000 = $90,000

   1.5% × $6,240,000 = $93,600

3. Receivables: Current

   $4,800,000 × (75/360) = $1,000,000

4. Receivables: Revised

   $5,760,000 × (80/360) = $1,280,000

   $6,000,000 × (80/360) = $1,333,333

   $6,240,000 × (80/360) = $1,386,667

382

	Aged analysis
	$
July	160
August	0
September	204
October	233
	————
	597
	————

July = AC212 $192 – CN92 $53 = $160

September = AC690

October = AC913

383 An aged analysis of receivables allows an entity to **focus its collection efforts to enforce its credit terms.** It makes it more obvious whether an increase/decrease in a balance is due to changed activity levels or a change in payment policy by a customer. This makes it easier for the company to assess whether it should carry on doing business, how it should **set credit limits** and whether it **needs to take any action in respect of large balances.**

384 The answer is **63 days.**

Raw materials inventory	$\dfrac{\text{Raw materials inventory}}{\text{Purchases}}$	111/641 × 365 =	63.2

385 The answer is **26 days.**

WIP inventory	$\dfrac{\text{Work in progress}}{\text{Cost of sales}}$	63/898 × 365 =	25.6

386 The answer is **41 days.**

Finished goods inventory	$\dfrac{\text{Finished goods inventory}}{\text{Cost of sales}}$	102/898 × 365 =	41.4

387 The answer is **80 days.**

Receivables days	$\dfrac{\text{Trade receivables}}{\text{Credit sales}}$	216/992 × 365 =	79.5

388 The answer is **55 days.**

Payables days	$\dfrac{\text{Payables}}{\text{Credit purchases}}$	97/641 × 365 =	55.2

389 The answer is **155 days.**

63 + 26 + 41 + 80 – 55 = 155 (answers as per Questions 383 to 387)

390 The answer is **1,041 units.**

$$EOQ = \sqrt{\frac{2cd}{h}}$$

Where   d   =   annual demand

           h   =   cost of holding one unit for one year

           c   =   cost of placing order

Therefore: $\sqrt{\dfrac{2 \times 25 \times 65,000}{3}} = 1,041$

391 The answer is a saving of **$12,312.**

Total cost using the EOQ of 1,041:	$
Purchase cost (65,000 × $10)	650,000.00
Procurement cost (65,000/1,041 = 63 orders × $25)	1,575.00
Holding cost (1,041/2 × $3)	1,561.50
Total annual costs	653,136.50

Total cost if order 2,000:	$
Purchase cost (65,000 × $9.80)	637,000.00
Procurement cost (65,000/2,000 = 33 orders × $25)	825.00
Holding cost (2,000/2 × $3)	3,000.00
Total annual costs	640,825.00

It is therefore worth increasing the order size as it will reduce costs by $12,311.50 a year.

392 The answer is **B, E and F.**

DF could obtain short-term finance from any of the following sources:

- by increasing the overdraft, however, **this is unlikely** as the overdraft is already quite high

- by taking out a short-term loan

- by taking additional credit from suppliers

 DF currently has trade payable days outstanding of 49 days (16/120 × 365). An increase of $2 million to $18 million would be 55 days (18/120 × 365), this needs to be viewed against the credit period offered by the suppliers. As the typical payables days are 45, the increase would **probably not be acceptable** and could cause problems obtaining future credit.

- by improving the receivables collection period:

 DF's trade receivables collection period is currently 30 days (20/240 × 365), which is quite low and in line with the industry average. **So this is unlikely to be a viable option** as it would involve reducing the trade receivables collection period to 27 days (18/240 × 365).

- by factoring or invoice discounting.

393 The most appropriate investment would be **the internet bank. Both investments are** considered to be low risk.

Bonds:

	$
Cost, including commission @ 1%	120,000

Cost less commission $120,000 × 100/101 = $118,812

Value on redemption 118,812 × 100/102	116,482
Interest @ 12.5% on 116,482	14,560
Net benefit	11,042

Internet bank:

Interest @ 0.8% per month – so there will be 12 interest periods during the year.

Value in 12 months' time = $120,000 (1 + 0.008)^{12}$ = $132,041

Net benefit = $12,041

The internet bank offers the most appropriate investment based on the return generated. As both investments are relatively low risk, return is an appropriate basis for the decision.

394 The answer is **B and C.**

395 The answer is **11%.**

The annual interest payable on the bond is $70 ($1,000 × 7%).

Calculate the internal rate of return of the relevant cash flows:

Time		CF	DF@7%	PV	DF@10%	PV
0	(MV)	(850)	1	(850)	1	(850)
1–5	I	70	4.100	287	3.791	265
5	R	1000	0.713	713	0.621	621
				150		36

Yield = IRR ≈ 7 + (10 – 7) × 150/(150 – 36) = approximately 11%.

Note: Alternative rates could be used but still produce an answer of approximately 11%.

396

Forms of short-term investments
Negotiable instruments
Short-term government bonds
Interest bearing bank accounts

The other items are types of short-term finance.

397

	Bank overdrafts	**Bank loans**
Advantage	Flexible	Fixed finance cost
Advantage	Generally cheaper	Repayment date known
Disadvantage	Repayable on demand	Generally more expensive
Disadvantage	Variable finance cost	Less flexible

398 The answer is **B and E.**

399 **B**

400 **D**

401 **C**